Charles Cornwallis Chesney

A Military View of Recent Campaigns in Virginia and Maryland

Charles Cornwallis Chesney

A Military View of Recent Campaigns in Virginia and Maryland

ISBN/EAN: 9783337813420

Printed in Europe, USA, Canada, Australia, Japan

Cover: Foto ©Suzi / pixelio.de

More available books at **www.hansebooks.com**

A MILITARY VIEW

OF

RECENT CAMPAIGNS

IN

VIRGINIA AND MARYLAND.

BY

Capt. C. C. CHESNEY, R.E.,
PROFESSOR OF MILITARY HISTORY, SANDHURST COLLEGE.

WITH MAPS.

LONDON:
SMITH, ELDER AND CO., 65, CORNHILL.

M.DCCC.LXIII.

TO

H.R.H. THE DUKE OF CAMBRIDGE,

UNDER WHOSE DIRECTION

THE STUDY OF MILITARY HISTORY HAS FIRST BEEN INTRODUCED

INTO THE EDUCATION OF THE BRITISH OFFICER,

THIS LITTLE WORK

IS (WITH HIS ROYAL HIGHNESS'S GRACIOUS PERMISSION)

MOST RESPECTFULLY DEDICATED BY

THE AUTHOR.

CONTENTS.

CHAP.		PAGE
I.	THE THEATRE OF WAR	1
II.	THE ARMIES AND THEIR LEADERS	13
III.	M'CLELLAN'S ADVANCE ON RICHMOND BY THE PENINSULA	22
IV.	RETREAT OF M'CLELLAN	59
V.	POPE'S CAMPAIGN IN VIRGINIA	76
VI.	THE INVASION OF MARYLAND AND FALL OF HARPER'S FERRY	101
VII.	BATTLE OF ANTIETAM.—LEE RETREATS INTO VIRGINIA	117
VIII.	THE FOURTH INVASION OF VIRGINIA.—M'CLELLAN SUPERSEDED	138
IX.	BURNSIDE'S CHANGE OF BASE	158
X.	FREDERICKSBURG	170
POSTSCRIPT.—CHANCELLORSVILLE		198

INTRODUCTION.

This book is not offered to the Public as a complete history of the campaigns of which it treats. The Author would consider the task of composing such a work to be greatly beyond his powers, even were it possible for him to have gathered already the necessary material.

But there is a peculiarity accompanying the whole progress of the American civil war, which enables it to be discussed in a way that no other such contest has been. For every phase of its greater events—at least of those occurring near the two capitals—has been witnessed and described by numerous observers of different nations, and of every class of opinion. And it is believed to be possible, whilst the subject is yet of present interest, to collect from existing sources such a narrative as shall put before the general reader all the really important matter, without wearying him with unnecessary details concerning unknown personages and doubtful events.

For this purpose, research has been made into numerous periodicals of France, England, Germany, and America, for the accounts given by eye-witnesses of the different operations here treated of. The Author has endeavoured to eliminate from these with care the colouring given by the passion of the day, or by extravagance of writing; so as to produce something as nearly approaching to a reliable history as the means afford. Such sources must necessarily abound in errors, but these he hopes will be here found corrected: for he has been favoured with numerous private communications from persons who have been spectators of portions of the war, or have had relatives actively engaged in it. He has also, by the kindness of some of them, had access to valuable correspondence bearing on its leading features down to the end of 1862.

In the last section—that on the operations in April and May, 1863, which has been written since the former portion went to the press—there has of necessity not been sufficient time to make the same close inquiries as to less certain points. The Author requests that this circumstance may be admitted as an apology for any minor inaccuracy that may be found in it: and he would take this opportunity of expressing his sincere thanks to the friends who have given him their help in gathering the materials for this, and assisted him essentially in preparing the former chapters.

The account here offered of M'Clellan's peninsular campaign is based upon the well-known and highly interesting work attributed to the French Princes. But that work leans (as is most natural) to the Federal side somewhat too strongly. The Author has had the advantage of correcting it in certain parts from the details furnished him by a friend, who went through all the same scenes as an impartial observer. He has also consulted some Confederate sources not available when the French account was written.

In reviewing the conduct of the different generals, under particular circumstances, it has been endeavoured to avoid all mere theorizing, and to support the remarks made upon them by illustrations drawn from the behaviour, under like conditions, of recognized masters of the military art. Without some such attempt to form a judgment, it is believed no critical account of any modern campaign would be of much value to the non-professional reader.

It is hoped that the accompanying sketches may enable any one, who is not provided with a better map, to follow the leading operations step by step. They have been prepared solely with reference to the work, and, for the purpose of clearness, all features of the country, but those actually needful, have been omitted.

RECENT CAMPAIGNS

IN

VIRGINIA AND MARYLAND.

CHAPTER I.

THE THEATRE OF WAR.

The inquiring reader of military history will usually find most pleasure and profit in studying campaigns and battles conducted by the great masters of the art of war. In their achievements he may trace not only the great principles of the art itself, but also see how wonderfully natural genius and matured judgment have varied their application under different circumstances. To follow closely the strategy of Napoleon —to trace out the tactical details of the battles of Hannibal—not only adds to our stock of knowledge, and exercises our critical powers; but it gratifies, as we rise to fuller comprehension of the workings of those great intellects, that craving for fit objects for hero-worship which is among the most universal of the passions our nature feels.

Yet there is no great operation of war but carries its lessons with it; and the last year's struggle around Richmond and Washington, even with our present imperfect knowledge of its details, presents an interesting subject for reflection. The almost constant reverses of the Northern army must have had their corresponding causes, we may safely assert. Nor are these far to seek: for we find on their side a divided command opposed to unity of action; masses of men in arms, without military *esprit* or discipline, meeting an army entitled to the name, by the subordinate spirit, as well as by the valour, of its soldiers; loud threats and idle bluster, encountered by calm firmness and steadfast endurance; finally, a contempt for the principles of war on the one hand, against a marked use of them on the other. This contempt, as will be hereafter seen, was loudly avowed by one of the Federal commanders as the true course to act upon: and it is interesting to observe that he soon found a practical application of those principles by his opponent, was the means of ruining himself, and driving his army in disgrace to take refuge behind the intrenchments of Washington, there to seek some more competent and less boastful leader.

A clear and succinct account of the opening of the American war, and the first operations,—those in Virginia being confined chiefly to the disastrous battle of Bull's Run, and the total repulse of the first advance of the Northerners on Richmond—was given to the public in a lecture delivered at the United Service Institution by Major Miller, V.C., and since published, both in the proceedings of the Institution and separately. To this the reader is referred for the details of that part of the conflict.

For the purpose of making our narrative clear, let us discard from our view the numerous mixed expeditions on the inland waters and on various parts of the Southern coast, as well as the guerilla warfare of the Border States, and the more important, yet desultory, struggle waged by the armies on the borders of Tennessee, Alabama, and Mississippi; and keep our attention on the operations conducted for the attack and defence of the Southern capital, which have been of the most vital interest as concerns the prospects of the Confederacy, and have chiefly attracted the notice of European observers.

The three objects originally laid out for the

Northern forces to achieve, being, as is now well known, (1) to blockade the sea coast of the Confederacy and prevent trade; (2) to open and keep command of the navigation of the Western rivers; and (3) to drive the Southern Government from its chosen seat at Richmond; and the two former having been in great part accomplished, it is the object of the present narrative to show why the Federals had, up to the end of 1862, made no more progress in the one remaining than on the unlucky day of July, 1861, when they were first advancing from Washington, under the command of M'Dowall, against the position of Manasses.

The theatre of that part of the war we have to follow should be examined with some attention. It lies between the Atlantic and the Alleghany Mountains, a steep chain rising to the height of 4,000 feet; and which, after roughly dividing North Carolina from Tennessee, enters Virginia, and passes through that old and historic state, forming a rugged backbone to it, crossed by a few very bad roads only, so that the two sections of the State are completely separated. Thence the chain is continued through a narrow part of the border State of Maryland, and loses itself in Pennsylvania. The division of Eastern and Western Virginia is not more complete geographically than it is in social and political feeling, for the majority of the inhabitants of the latter section, a race of comparatively recent settlers, incline to the cause of the North; whilst East Virginia, with which we have had to deal, is known as the very heart of the aristocratic element of the Southern States. But these two sections, taken strictly, do not comprise the whole of Virginia. Parallel to the Alleghanies, at a distance of about sixty miles to the east, run the Blue Mountains, a similar but lesser chain. The long valley enclosed by these two ranges, and drained by the river Shenandoah, is remarkable for its picturesque beauty, being much broken by lesser ridges, and was, until war brought ruin on its thriving farmers, as noted for its agricultural wealth. The inhabitants, descended from emigrants of an early date, have shown throughout the struggle a strong sympathy for the Southern cause.

Eastern Virginia is separated from Maryland by that important river the Potomac, which, descending from the Alleghanies, and flowing in a generally south-eastern direction, separates the Blue Mountains from their continuation in Maryland and Pennsylvania, known as the South Mountain, and finally loses itself in the waters of Chesapeake Bay. On its way it receives the Shenandoah at Harper's Ferry, and a number of other much less important streams from the Virginia side, one of the last being the famous Bull's Run, or Occocquan.

The Shenandoah, it should be remarked, is of considerable size through much of its course, and, as it flows between deep banks, and from the nature of the country round it is liable to sudden and violent floods, it forms a very serious obstacle to an army operating across the valley. Many tributaries reach the Potomac from the Maryland side: the most important of these for us to note being the Monocacy, which passes by Frederic City, the capital of the State; and Antietam Creek, now of such historic note. Both of these rise in the hilly district of central Pennsylvania—a tract of country formed by the northern spurs of the Alleghanies and other attendant ridges—and flow nearly due south; the former to the east, the latter to the west of the South Mountain. The Potomac is navigable for vessels of light draught up to Washington, and the chief port on it is Alexandria, a small town on the southern bank. This place, though on the opposite side to the capital, and also lower down the stream, is near enough to it to have been made the proper terminus for the railroad, which, before the war, was the main artery of communication from Washington, through Eastern Virginia, to Richmond, and thence on to the more southern Atlantic States.

The Blue Ridge and the hills adjacent give rise to numerous streams, which make their way, on the west side, of course, into the Shenandoah, but on the east converge into certain main rivers which flow across Eastern Virginia into the Chesapeake. Of these the most noteworthy are the Rappahannock, navigable nearly up to Fredericsburg, an old Virginian town, and the chief place on it; and the James, fifty miles farther south, on the northern bank of which, and nearly at the head of its navigation, is Richmond. The lower or tidal part of this latter is wide and deep; and not many miles to its north, a large and long creek, forming an outlet for the Pamunkey and some lesser streams, and running in a parallel direction, under the name of York River, leaves a remarkable peninsula between itself and the James. This peninsula begins about forty miles east of Richmond, is about fifty long, and varies from twenty to a much lesser breadth in places. At its seaward extremity lies Fort Monroe, a strong place held by the Federals since the war first began, and looking into Hampton Roads, where the James meets the sea. Here also ends the Elizabeth River, a very few miles up which is the naval arsenal of Norfolk, for many months held by the Southerners.

It is not merely the direction of the rivers in Eastern Virginia which impedes an army advancing from Washington on Richmond; but the nature of the country—which is of a very undulating surface, of a heavy soil, sparsely populated according to European ideas, and broken by large masses of virgin forest—presents other difficulties of a most formidable nature. Add to these, that the roads, so called, are not made roads in the accepted sense of the term, but mere tracks over the surface, sure to be rendered impassable by rainy weather, combined with any considerable amount of traffic; and it would seem that the mere transport, by their means, of an army of magnitude, even if unopposed, over the 150 miles which lie between the two capitals, would be a physical impossibility, save under the condition of the very finest weather being secured for the whole period of the operation. The rashest general whom the Lincoln Cabinet could have selected would scarcely have proposed to attempt the advance, except in reliance on the supply of his army by railroad communication.

As the railroads of this part of America have advanced to a degree of usefulness and completeness, far out of proportion, to judge by a European standard, to that of the ordinary roads, so in the late campaigns their importance has been most remarkably shown. Let us here examine the course of those most available for purposes of offence and defence as regards the rival capitals; premising generally, that American railroads are usually of a very rough and ready description as compared with European ones; are composed of single lines with occasional sidings, and rude uninclosed stations; have much timber-work in the more difficult parts; and are, therefore, easily broken up, and also easily restored.

Mention has been already made of a main line from Washington southwards. This, under the name of the Orange and Alexandria Railroad, leaves the latter town on the Potomac with a south-westerly course, passing no place of importance for its whole length to Orange Courthouse, which is just south of the Rappahannock. Continued beyond this to Gordonsville, it there meets the Virginia Central Railroad coming from the west by Staunton in the Upper Shenandoah valley, which carries it into Richmond by making a southern bend for the last twenty miles of its course. A second communication between the rival capitals is by descending the Potomac to Acquia Creek, whence a straight line of seventy miles, running due south, and crossing the Rappahannock at Fredericksburg, conducts direct to Richmond. A short straight line leads east from Richmond to the Pamunkey at Whitehouse, whence there is a free communication seawards for small vessels by the York River. To the south of Richmond traffic is conducted from the city not only by James River, but by two railroads, one running southwards by Petersburg and Weldon along the coast line of the Carolinas, and the other more westerly, by Lynchburg, in the direction of East Tennessee.

The lower part of the Shenandoah valley is entered either from Harper's Ferry, whence a railroad leads to Winchester, the chief town of the northern portion; or from the Alexandria line, whence a branch, turning off at a junction about twenty-five miles from Washington, is led with much engineering skill over the Blue Ridge by the pass called Manasses Gap, first crossing an outlying range of high hills, called in this part the Bull's Run Mountain, by Thoroughfare Gap. This line having entered the valley and reached a place called Front Royal, turns southward as far as the town of Mount Jackson, crossing on its way the north and south forks of the Shenandoah by considerable bridges.

There is a short railroad from Alexandria along

the southern bank of the Potomac in the direction of Harper's Ferry, but carried no farther than the town of Leesburg, where it meets the northern end of the Blue Ridge. Running nearly along what was the line of separation of the hostile territories in the earlier part of the war, it appears to have been little if at all used, and may be left out of our view.

A single railroad forms the approach from the work to Washington, after the traveller going southwards has reached the city of Baltimore. A branch from this line to Annapolis, on the higher part of the Chesapeake, was the only means, other than the waters of the Potomac, that the Northerners had of reaching their capital, and the base of their future operations, during the brief space at the beginning of the war, when the mob of Baltimore interfered with the passage of the volunteer regiments from New England through that city to Washington. Hence the necessity for that strong military occupation of this important point, which the Federal forces have ever since maintained.

From Baltimore the northern traffic is carried by two main lines of railroad. A third line, the Baltimore and Ohio, leaves the city for the west; passes near Frederic, the official capital of Maryland; thence makes for the Potomac, which it meets at a place called Point of Rocks; continues up the northern bank of the river to Harper's Ferry, where it crosses, and sends off the Winchester branch, already mentioned, up the Shenandoah valley; then follows up the line of the Potomac, making its way to the sources of that stream, and through the Alleghany Mountains into the great central State of Ohio. Any one point of this great artery occupied by the Southerners, necessarily interrupts all direct communication between Washington and the middle States.

Having thus examined the features of the country in which the late campaigns were carried on, and the communications likely to be available for the use of the hostile commanders, it remains to consider briefly the composition and character of the forces on either side, and their bearings on the events that have occurred.

CHAPTER II.

THE ARMIES AND THEIR LEADERS.

RAISED by the application of the volunteer* principle in its widest sense, and from among a people whose traditions of war naturally caused them to put perfect faith in it, the Northern army has, by its uniform ill-success, thrown some degree of undeserved discredit on that principle. Many of those who have criticised the disasters of 1862, suffered by the rapidly extemporized Federal forces, forget that the whole army of Great Britain is essentially an army of volunteers. Voluntary enlistment by bounty cannot of itself be the vice which has caused these disasters,

* It may be observed that the remarks here apply solely to the raising of armies for general service to the State. It is not the place to discuss the value of those bodies organized specially for purposes of defence. But the writer has had some personal knowledge of the system of French National Guards in the days of the Citizen King, and later of that of the American militia in time of peace, and of the Prussian reserves, and can safely assert that our present splendid body of volunteers is, in all points that make efficiency, infinitely the superior of any of these.

for no one has ever asserted the English recruit to be in any way inferior, as raw material, to the conscript of the Continent.

The fact is that the principle we are commenting on was shamefully abused when the Federal army was raised. A mass of locally formed battalions, got together by the exertions of the petty political leaders of districts, officered by men in no way superior to those they commanded, the commissions being bestowed by the State governors through their creatures as the price of party support,—the Federal army contained in its every company the seeds of envy, discontent, and insubordination. The higher commissions to the rank of brigadier-general were lavished at first in a way still more surprising on some of the most incompetent of those who left the store and counting-house for the new and popular trade. No liberal scale of bounty or pay, no national enthusiasm, no energy in the Government, could supply the place of that respect for their leaders, and that ready following out of superior orders which was here wholly wanting, and without which an army is but an armed and dangerous mob. Add to this vice of original formation, that the endeavour was made in the beginning to organize and employ a force of such battalions as these without any general staff—that is, without any general directing power,—and we have the elements, if there be any truth in history, of certain failure in any attempt at offensive movements. Indeed, up to the present time, though defeat has forced on many improvements (as a certain examination* of the officers appointed), and time has been given amply sufficient for perfect training, the army has not emerged from the consequences of these first errors. These, and the democratic spirit general throughout the ranks, make the Federal forces untrustworthy in the field to a degree quite astonishing to those who know the individual fitness of the mass of American recruits for the service of war.

To go back to a special period. In March, 1862, we find an army of 130,000 of these volunteers assembled round Washington, under General M'Clellan. This officer, like most of those distinguished on either side for any practical efficiency in this war, had enjoyed a full theoretical training in the Westpoint Academy, the maintenance of which, in a very complete condition, has long been a marked exception to the niggardly dealings of the United States with their

---

* An examination of the officers of State regiments by a regular board was instituted by Congress in the spring of 1862. Loose as the system of working this in practice is, its introduction caused a perceptible improvement. In M'Clellan's peninsular army alone 110 of the most ignorant officers were at once got rid of when the order for the examination was received!

regular forces. Brought hastily into command of the Northern army after the disaster of Bull's Run; reaping the advantage of the panic of those days in large powers and strong support from the terrified Government; in the prime of life, and having had (during his appointment as military commissioner in the Crimea) some previous knowledge of the difficulties of a great war; the new general was as likely as any other man available to carry out the allotted task of welding together, and leading to victory, the rude mass of volunteers placed under him. And he developed a considerable talent for the organizing branch of his art. Not being required (as was his unlucky predecessor M'Dowall,) to manage a large army without any assistance but that of two aides-de-camp, he had formed a regular imitation of the divisional system of a modern European army, to which were added by degrees the needful adjuncts of military, commissariat, and medical staffs, transport corps, and such like. More than this, he had attracted to himself, in a very striking degree, the confidence and affection of his soldiery—so completely so, that these clung to him through his most evil fortunes. Unhappily, whilst these things were being done, the necessary delays had roused the impatience of the Northern press, and this, reacting on the Cabinet, had gradually diminished the influence of the general with the Government, at the very time when it was essential to success that harmony should be fully maintained. In this rising want of confidence in the leader chosen by themselves, and the interference of the Cabinet with his plans in consequence, were the elements of great disasters to come. For the rest, though scarcely past the rudimentary drills, and quite untrained in real field movements, the troops were well equipped and clothed, and were accompanied by a very formidable artillery. It must be added, that the staff was as yet inadequate in number and skill to their duties; and that, owing greatly to the neglect of riding exercise in the Northern States, the cavalry were few and bad beyond any precedent in so large an army.

The Southern army covering Richmond against the expected advance of M'Clellan was scarcely half his strength, and inferior by far in equipment. In common with the other Confederate forces, it had been formed originally of State volunteer regiments, by a process not very dissimilar to that which was employed in the North. But from the very first the South had enjoyed the special advantage, derived from her aristocratically composed society, of a class of men accustomed to command and lead others.

These gave her officers whom the privates could respect; and her Government, more far-seeing and more powerful than that of the Federals, soon succeeded in securing the whole commissioning of the army above the rank of second lieutenant, and thus founding an improved military organization. To this a stringent Conscription Bill being added, a supply of soldiers was secured without that enormous expenditure of bounties employed in the North. The spirit of the men was excellent, for the prestige of victory from the autumn was united with the patriotic feeling roused by the loud threats of their enemies; and these were aided by a confidence in their generals, who were nearly all distinguished pupils of Westpoint. That college, and some of a more private character maintained by certain of the States, had always been more frequented by Southerners than by the sons of the more commercial North, and the cause of Secession now reaped great benefit from this difference of taste. More than 300 old *élèves* of Westpoint, and many more from State military colleges, took up arms at once for the cause of Secession, and greatly assisted the construction of the new army and its military establishments. The immense exertions of officers, formerly in the United States' Artillery, were gradually supplying the deficiencies in that arm. In cavalry the Confederates were better off than their opponents, for the South had preserved the practice of horsemanship, and many of her better class were well mounted. In this arm, so much needed the previous year to complete the victory of Bull's Run, they had organized a considerable force, and a leader, Stuart, had been found for them from among the younger officers of Westpoint training, who seems to have been most perfectly qualified to carry the usefulness of light troops of that branch to the utmost limit: his recent services, in covering his own army and harassing the enemy's, have earned him a foremost name in the list of cavalry leaders.

General Joseph Johnson* commanded the Southern army of Virginia. A man of mature age, like his namesake (also of the old cavalry service) who led the Confederates in the West till he fell at Pittsburg, and much older than his opponent M'Clellan, he had served originally in the Engineers, but left that branch of the army for the Dragoons, and had attained the rank of lieutenant-colonel when the war broke out. His former service in Mexico, and his well-known high character as a scientific soldier, had placed him in an important command from the very

* This general's name is spelt *Johnson* in the present despatches of the Confederate War Department, but stands as *Johnston* in the old United States' Army List.

first. He it was who brought from the Shenandoah Valley the troops who arrived through Manasses Gap in time to turn the struggle at Bull's Run into a complete victory. He soon after succeeded Beauregard, his former junior in the old service, and under whom he had cheerfully acted in the battle, in the charge of the forces who were still to threaten Washington and guard Richmond. Uniting in a remarkable degree the ardour and activity of youth to the matured judgment of sixty years, he fully justified the sagacity of the Government which had chosen him for their most important command.

He had an army of about 60,000 men under his immediate control, most of which had been lying in the old position in front of Manasses Gap Junction ever since the Southerners had abandoned their posts close to Washington to fall back nearer to their supplies. There were also detached forces in the Shenandoah Valley, on the peninsula near Richmond, about the dockyard of Norfolk, and on the coasts of North Carolina. All these were employed in observing various desultory expeditions directed by the Federals in these different quarters. But the central position of Richmond as regarded all of these, promised the Confederate war department the facility of uniting their whole forces near that capital without the possibility of their enemies interfering with the operation, and of thus employing what is called in technical phrase "the advantage of interior lines" in case of any formidable attempt against it.

The staff of their army, however, and the general discipline of the soldiery, were scarcely more adequate than those of the North to the carrying out of the complicated operations of strategy in a perfect way. Their transport, much required to supplement the use of the railroads, was very deficient. These defects known, it might be presumed that, however superior their conceptions might be to those of their foes— however great the advantages gained in the field—it would be impossible to reap from either those full results which alone could give a triumphant peace, such as European armies, with their greater facilities and better training for following up victory, have often won by a single successful campaign.

Having thus taken our survey of the various conditions under which the operations of 1862 were opened, we proceed to follow the events in due course.

CHAPTER III.

M'CLELLAN'S ADVANCE ON RICHMOND BY THE PENINSULA.

DOUBTLESS during the long six months passed by M'Clellan in organizing the army of the Potomac, he often revolved the difficulties which beset each choice of means to accomplish the task laid before him. The direct advance on Richmond, for which the Northern journals shouted loudly, he knew to involve a slow and painful advance through a hostile country, with but one line of supplies, the Orange Railroad, and that liable to be constantly interrupted by the flank incursions of an enemy known to be thoroughly acquainted with the country. It was evident that if the foe yielded to this advance, and retired without battle, they would have singular advantages in impeding his pursuit by the destruction of the railroad bit by bit, and by the defence of the various rivers crossing it from west to east.

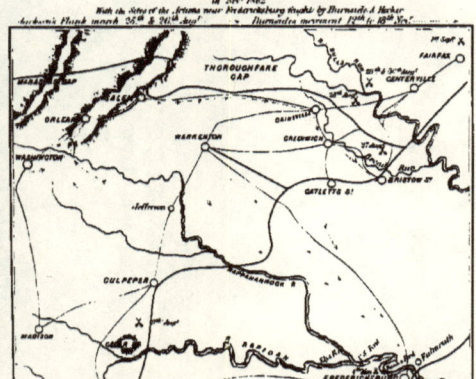
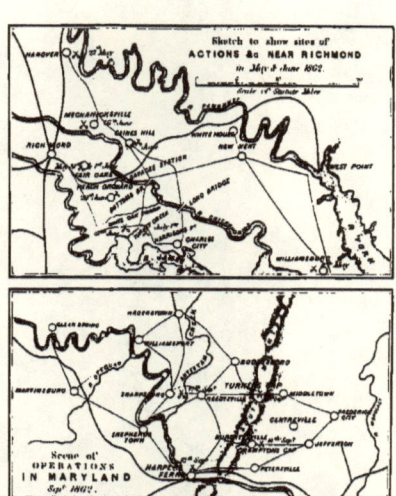

He devised, therefore, a different plan. Washington had been early begun to be surrounded by strong field intrenchments, and these were carried on still on a mighty scale, as if not only to shelter the capital from sudden surprise, but also to form a strong fortified base whence the army could advance southward, with a perfectly safe point to fall back upon, if need were. Such had been the strategy of the great duke when he formed the lines of Torres Vedras round Lisbon, and it would appear no shame to imitate his example. But M'Clellan had another use for these intrenchments. He would forsake Washington as his base for a time, when the army should be ready and the winter gone, and leaving only a garrison in the lines, would avail himself of the unequalled water transport he could call for, and carry his invading host down the Potomac, to land near Richmond. Their great unwieldiness and huge wants would not enable him to take them far from the ships; a day's march inland would leave them in want, it was feared; but the waters of York and James rivers might be used to bring them all that was needed until Richmond fell, and the Confederates had no known means of interfering with such mode of operation until he should come within striking distance of their capital.

To carry out this design fully, it was necessary to

keep the Confederate army near Washington, in order to anticipate them by the sea move, when they became alarmed for Richmond. For this the utmost secrecy was needful, but here treason interfered; and as soon as M'Clellan made known his design and the reasons of his delay to his generals of division, the news reached his foes also. On the 9th March he had the mortification of learning that the latter had broken up their camp at Manasses, and were retreating to the south, having evidently in some degree fathomed his design. An attempt, which was made on the spur of the moment, to follow up and close with the Confederates only served to show that the passage through Eastern Virginia was, owing to the swelling of the streams by winter rains, more difficult even than was supposed; and further, that a single line of railroad would prove, even if in perfect order, hardly adequate to the numerous wants of the Northern host. Their huge demands upon the commissariat here already placed them at a disadvantage with the Southern army, who from the first had been compelled to do their work upon moderate or even scanty rations.

M'Clellan was doomed to more serious mortifications than even the disclosure of his plan. Even while he had scarce resolved to attempt to carry it out without the advantage of surprise, the support on which he had reckoned, the authority with which he had been clothed, fell from him. The growing impatience of his delay turned the minds of the Cabinet against him, and a hostile Secretary for War had now influence enough to strip him of the chief command of the Union land forces, held by him since the retirement of the veteran Scott some months before. On the 11th an order appeared which, under pretence of reorganizing the armies, reduced M'Clellan to the actual charge of that operating in Virginia, then consisting of eleven divisions of volunteers, each averaging about 10,000 infantry, and divided into three brigades of four battalions : these, with a very powerful artillery numbering 350 pieces light and heavy, a small division of the regular army, and a few regiments of indifferent cavalry, made up the 130,000 before mentioned.

But even of this force he was no longer allowed to dispose after his own fashion. Instead of leaving future promotion of the higher officers to depend in any way on him, it was now, without or against his will, divided into four *corps d'armée*, placed under the senior generals present—Sumner, Keyes, M'Dowall, and Heintzelman. M'Dowall had commanded at Washington at the first, and had, some time since his supersession, been raised to the rank of major-general. But the other three were brigadier-generals only, and had lately been doing duty as field officers of the old army in common with most of the other division generals, from whom they were in no real way separated, the seniority being, in the first hasty promotions of Lincoln, matter of chance or interest. The new organization into corps, if a good form in itself, introduced indeed by Napoleon, was here ordered so as to remove the other generals from any direct responsibility to, or communication with, M'Clellan, and much diminished his personal authority. To further add to his difficulties, the garrisons of Washington and of Fortress Monroe, the very two points one of which he must needs select as the base and depôt of future operations, were placed under commanders independent of him altogether; and his army was weakened at the very moment of its departure by the withdrawal of a whole division, Blenker's, taken from him to go under Fremont, the new favourite of the hour, to wander uselessly along the slopes of the Alleghanies.

Notwithstanding these various discouragements, to be followed by still more serious weakening of his army hereafter, and in spite of delay and insufficiency of the transports he had long since called for, M'Clellan proceeded steadily in the execution of his design. Huge river steamers, each carrying the sort of floating hotel or barrack in which the American traveller delights, bore his battalions down the broad Chesapeake to Fortress Monroe; and on the 3rd April we find the general himself landing and pushing his forces onward up the peninsula. But he no longer has the choice of the James or York Rivers for the transport of his daily supplies and the action of the gunboats to guard his flank; for on the very day (9th March) on which he had made his futile advance on Manasses, the celebrated "first battle of the iron-clads" had taken place in Hampton Roads, and the formidable *Merrimac*, though for the time repulsed, still lay at Norfolk, watching her opportunity to issue forth and deal destruction among the frail transports and their living freight. To her was opposed the *Monitor*, which had before driven her off, aided by strong and swift wooden steamers, manned by a few resolute men, prepared to run her down at the risk of sacrificing their own lives and vessels; and these precautions, with the impediments sunk in the channels by the navy, had the desired effect of restraining the monster from her threatened attack. But it was deemed too hazardous to make the army dependent on a line of water transport, the flank of which was so exposed to this dreaded enemy, and it remained, therefore, only to M'Clellan to use the York River and the Pamunkey for his boats, and afterwards the York River railroad in his advance upon Richmond.

Led by General Keyes' corps, the army had made scarce two days' march, when they were arrested by the lines of Yorktown running clear across the peninsula at a narrow part of it. A few miserable houses at the eastern end of the works occupied the site of the old settlement famous in the history of the United States for the surrender of Cornwallis. No reading in the history of England's wars is more painful than that which tells the tale of the brave single-hearted soldier who there maintained, till borne down by hopeless odds, the honour of his country's flag. Now calling in vain for aid on his inert and distant chief—now striving to tempt his wary foe to action upon such open ground as might give British discipline its advantage—now strengthening his feeble defences as the enemy accumulated their overwhelming forces by land and sea—he taught his faithful band to hope against hope to the last, yielded only when defence was possible no longer, and spent the last hours of his freedom in providing for the safety of the loyal colonists who had joined their fortunes to his own. Cornwallis at Yorktown shows us plainly that the race which produced the heroes of Lucknow and Delhi did not want its representative even among the blunders and disgraces of the American revolutionary war.

But the lines of 1862 were not merely, as those of 1781, thrown up to enclose a strip of land on the York River shore. They crossed, as has been said, the whole neck of the peninsula. Guarded in front by creeks and inundations, mounted with guns of the heaviest calibre, and held by 12,000 men (reported as 20,000) under Magruder, an old officer of a character bold and determined to the point of rashness, here was an obstacle which threatened to bring M'Clellan's project to an end ere it was well begun. Moreover, the gunboats, far from being able to turn the flank of the enemy's lines, found so heavy a battery bearing on York River, and that so crossed with the fire of Fort Gloucester, a work thrown up on the north bank, that they reported it useless to attempt to force their way.

We must suppose, from later knowledge of the truth, that had M'Clellan known the smallness of Magruder's force—quite inadequate to the defence of the great length of his lines—and tried a combined assault upon their weaker portions, they must have fallen at once. But he believed the exaggerated estimate given (on this as on so many occasions) of the Confederate numbers, confirmed as it was by the bold front which Magruder, much to his credit, displayed; and he acted accordingly with that extreme caution which seems to form the blot on his character as a commander in the field. He had had some intimation of the opposition to be met with at this point. His plan to overcome it had been arranged beforehand, and seemed feasible enough. M'Dowall's corps, being the last in order of leaving Washington, was to be transported, not to the end of the peninsula, but to the opposite shore of York River. Moving along this, they would be able to turn and take the works at Gloucester, and so enable the gunboats to make their way up the stream. The very possibility that the Northerners might thus land forces on the line of retreat from Yorktown, would compel Magruder, it was thought, to a precipitate abandonment of the entrenchments thus threatened in rear.

Unhappily, the first step in this project was not taken, and that by no fault of the general. The President about this time seeing the mass of men who had long lain round Washington moving so rapidly off, and finding his capital covered by only the intrenchments and some 20,000 soldiers, grew— it would plainly appear from his own correspondence—

timid as to his own position. Haunted with visions of the advance of a Southern army strong enough to drive him from the White House, he took upon himself to retain M'Dowall's three divisions on the line of the Potomac. M'Clellan's remonstrances procured the despatch to his own aid of one of these three—Franklin's, commanded by an active officer of former service in whom he had much confidence; but the single division was not thought equal by the somewhat cautious commander to the work which had been laid out for the whole corps, and the design upon Gloucester was abandoned. An attempt to surprise an entrance into the Yorktown lines by wading a body of troops over part of the inundation was made on the 16th April, and failed; and it now remained only to drive the enemy from their defences by the slow and laborious process of regular siege works.

This was no easy matter, for Johnson had now assumed the command of the Confederates, and with him additional troops arrived, while his enemies allowed that his presence was a reinforcement of itself to the defenders. Well knew they the activity and readiness of the man they had before them, for not very long before he had been lieutenant-colonel to Sumner himself. Strange change of places, and strange meeting in a most strange and unnatural conflict! However, the attack was pressed, and the Northern army, by its aptitude for rough engineering work, and for adapting itself to the business of a siege camp, gained the admiration of European lookers-on. M'Clellan's magnificent train of heavy guns were now being brought into play, and he flattered himself their fire would soon cover a successful general assault on the lines, followed, it might be, by some considerable advantage on pressing the Confederates in their expected retreat. To do this the more effectually, Franklin's division was kept on board the transports ready to be landed at any point higher up the river on the Confederate flank.

But it was no part of Johnson's plan to run any such risk at present as a general action. The defences of Richmond on the east side had now been strengthened, and reinforcements ordered into them, whilst the Northern forces had suffered considerably from their month of detention in an exposed and marshy encampment. The Confederates therefore broke up on the night of the 3rd May, and retreated, having made all arrangements beforehand so completely that their enemy, on entering the deserted lines, found nothing but seventy of the heaviest guns, which they had been unable to carry with them. General Stoneman with the Federal cavalry was sent at once in pursuit; but only came up with the rearguard as they passed into a new entrenched position, from the approach to which the Federal cavalry, with their light guns accompanying, were driven off by a heavy fire, after a gallant but useless attempt to force their way in with the enemy's retreating infantry.

The point they had reached was fifteen miles from Yorktown, and near the little town of Williamsburg, the chief place on the peninsula. Two very deep creeks here running in from the opposite shores contracted the land to a mere neck of firm ground; so that the two roads which the Federals were approaching by, in their advance from the different extremities of the lines just taken, met in one, and so ran on to the town. A strong earthwork of regular *enceinte* closed the road and ground near it, and some lesser redoubts detached from this were intended to flank and prevent any attempt made to turn it. The whole seemed to be well armed and garrisoned, and night closed gloomily on the Northern advance, with the prospect of another long and wearisome delay before them. To add to their annoyance, Stoneman had lost one of his light guns carried rashly too near the Confederate works, and which the softness of the ground, and the heavy fire from the redoubts, rendered it impossible to recover.

On the morning of the 5th, M'Clellan, hampered by his great difficulty, the transport of his train, was still in the rear of his main columns; and General Sumner, the senior officer in the front of the army, proceeded to attempt the attack of the works. The battle of Williamsburg, as it has been called, ensued, and exemplified, in a striking manner, that entire want of cohesion in the movements of the Federals which has been observed in all their subsequent engagements, and which may be unhesitatingly attributed to their neglect to create an efficient general staff. Each commander threw his troops against the enemy in such manner, and at such time and place, as seemed to him the best, and the unity so necessary to complete success was utterly wanting. Heintzelman, advancing by the left (or west) road against the works with his two divisions under Hooker and Kearney, excellent and tried officers, commenced the attack from an early hour with the former. The Confederates repulsed him, and followed up their success into the woods from which the Northern army was emerging; but here they were checked by Kearney's men, whom their chief, an active battle-loving soldier (who, since distinguishing himself in Mexico, had served in

Africa and Italy under the French colours,) led on with such personal daring as to inspire courage in all who saw him. This combat, desultory from the tangled nature of the ground, had continued for some hours before Sumner could succeed in bringing aid from the road on the Federal right. At last a division was detached across to Hooker's assistance, whilst Hancock's brigade crossed the creek beyond the Confederate left at an unguarded point, and, having driven off the troops the enemy moved against them by a most gallant bayonet charge—a very rare feature in the uncertain, cautious tactics of American battles —held their position until M'Clellan, who arrived in the afternoon, was enabled to support them by some of the later arrivals of his long columns. Night and rain closed the contest, but the success of the Federals was decisive for the next day, as their army, deploying by the passage Hancock had won, would completely turn the enemy's works. Johnson therefore withdrew his army in the night, and moved rapidly on to his fortifications at Richmond, repulsing on his way (7th May) a feeble attempt against his flank made by Franklin's division, which had been carried up York River, and landed near the mouth of the Pamunkey.

On the 6th, M'Clellan occupied Williamsburg, where the Confederate general had left many sick and wounded. These, as well as those of the inhabitants who had not fled before the invaders, received excellent treatment. The conduct of this Northern army, which was marked in its forbearance towards the persons and property of the residents throughout the campaigns on the peninsula, may have been owing rather to the good morale of the better class of volunteers, and to the striking example of their commander and his staff, than to any strictness of discipline. At any rate, it presents a most favourable contrast to the excesses committed in Tennessee and Alabama during the same year, when every rule by which modern generals have softened the rigours of war has been thrown aside; when soldiers have been encouraged by their officers to plunder, excess, and cruelty; and the horrors of the Thirty Years' War have been revived, to the disgrace of the boasted civilisation of our age.

The Confederates having marched so swiftly in their retreat as to draw out of M'Clellan's sight altogether on the first day of their march, and quite to elude any useful pursuit, he now deliberately made every preparation for pushing his forces to their capital in irresistible strength. For the purpose of always keeping within a few hours of his supplies, he directed his march up the York River to the Pamunkey, and then followed the course of that stream, carefully exploring it in advance by the aid of his gunboats, until he brought his army, on the 16th May, to White House, the highest point that the vessel could reach. This place takes its name from a mansion formerly the residence of Washington, and lately that of General Lee, destined soon to distinction as Confederate commander-in-chief, and the head of a family descended from the wife * of the great founder of American independence. The house, it should be added, was scrupulously respected by M'Clellan's own care, until it was burnt down in the confusion of the retreat.

From White House the York River Railroad leads direct to Richmond. The Federals found the repair of it easy, and from this time used it for the supply of their army, forming a huge depot at the point where it leaves the Pamunkey. They advanced without further opposition or difficulty, and crossed the Chickahominy, a swampy stream flowing through heavy meadow land round the north of Richmond, and running south-east into the James. The point of crossing of the main turnpike road is called Bottom's Bridge, and the advance was now within ten miles of the desired object, but there were many

* Martha Custis, the widow whom Washington married. Lee married her grand-daughter.

signs that it would not be attained without a severe struggle.

In fact the Confederate forces had now begun to collect for the purpose of defending their capital, and striking a decisive blow at its assailant. Norfolk was abandoned, and the *Merrimac* blown up, in order to bring in General Huger and the large garrison— 18,000 men according to report—who had lain on the Elizabeth River. The force that had been guarding the coasts of North Carolina against the expedition of Burnside mysteriously disappeared from his front, and were heard of as near Richmond. It was even feared that some of the Confederate forces in Tennessee might be brought over to act against M'Clellan, for the Northern armies in that region seemed to have been paralysed, ever since the narrow escape of Grant from destruction at Pittsburg Landing in the great battle of the 6th and 7th April. It was evident, moreover, that General Jackson, who guarded the Shenandoah Valley for the Southerners, might move to Richmond before the forces opposed to him could follow, or go round to meet him. M'Clellan's situation, therefore, was an anxious one, and the more so, as any further progress towards the city must be made by the right or southern bank of the Chickahominy, whilst to guard his communications from Bottom's Bridge to the Pamunkey, he must needs keep much of his army on the other; and a continuation of heavy rains had swollen the stream, and turned the land along it into a difficult morass, so as to make the bridging it a very serious task.

To balance this evil the James River was now open to the Northerners since the *Merrimac* no longer existed, and it might ere long be made available for their transports. Indeed, an attempt had been made on the 16th to force the iron-clads up to the city itself, but they had been decisively repulsed by the works thrown up at Fort Darling, eight miles from Richmond : below this point they held the whole of the stream.

But M'Clellan did not at this time look to their operations for assistance to his own. He inclined rather to extend his right, and give the hand to an anticipated movement of M'Dowall's in co-operation with his own advance up the Chickahominy. The latter general, retained, as we have seen, by the personal will of the President, in the neighbourhood of Washington, with two divisions, had moved these, with some additions given him, into the Rappahannock district, which he held as a separate command. He had occupied Fredericksburg unopposed, and pushed outposts southward on the line of the railroad, which, as we know, runs direct from that town to Richmond. He had shown, by the honourable feeling with which he had worked for months under M'Clellan's orders, that he felt no touch of unworthy jealousy at his supersession by that commander after the Bull's Run disaster. The army before Richmond learning that he was within forty miles of their right flank, M'Clellan's immediate operations were directed to facilitate a communication and consequent junction.

For this purpose he detached the troops of Porter, his favourite general (formerly an artillerist); for whom, with Franklin, another officer in whom he put great confidence, he had just created special commands by a subdivision of his army into six corps, instead of the four originally formed. They marched on the night of the 27th May upon Hanover Courthouse, a station on the Virginia Central Railroad, twenty miles north of Richmond, where that line reaches the Pamunkey. A division of the Confederates guarded this point, covering both the line in question, and that to Fredericksburg, which runs very near it rather more to the west. General Branch, who commanded here, appears to have allowed himself to be surprised. Porter engaged him briskly in front, and at the same time moved a brigade on his flank through some thick cover; and after a short resistance the Confederates fled in much confusion, leaving about 400 prisoners, and suffering much in their flight from the fire of a light battery which followed them some distance.

This success appeared at once to give M'Clellan command of the whole of the communications of his enemy with the north part of Virginia, and the means of his own immediate junction with M'Dowall. But the high hopes thus raised in the breast of the Federal commander were dashed at once to the ground. The telegraph brought word that M'Dowall had been suddenly called in to defend Washington, and ordered M'Clellan to destroy the bridges which he commanded in the direction of Fredericksburg, that they might not be available for some anticipated move of the enemy against the former city. Thus we find Lincoln, whilst his chief army and best general are scarce more than cannon-shot from the lines round Richmond, trembling at the thought of Washington being taken. Let us see what caused this new fit of alarm, this worse than Aulic-Council-meddling with the operations of the unhappy Federal commanders.

Reference has been made before to a Confederate force in the Shenandoah Valley under General Jackson, an officer noted at the very beginning of the war for the admirable conduct of his brigade at Bull's Run, and for his share in directing the bloody repulse of the Federals in their attempt to cross the Potomac near Leesburg. Known at Westpoint for his reserved and quiet manner, and in later years (he was commissioned from that college in 1846) for activity and ability in the brief Mexican war; in peace he had shown apparent heaviness of temperament and a disposition to eccentricity and hypochondria, which had hindered his popularity at the State military college of Virginia, where he had been recently employed. The fierce excitement of the civil struggle brought out in him qualities which have attracted and bound the devotion of his soldiers to him in a most remarkable degree. Living just as one of his privates in habits and comfort; avoiding all state as well as luxury; teaching those around him to regard their cause as specially protected by heaven; leading the prayer-meeting, or administering the sacrament as Presbyterian elder; and dividing his spare hours between his Bible and his field-map— not the least remarkable result of this great strife has been the appearance of a leader who seems to combine the habits of Suwarrow with the self-discipline of Cromwell, and to be trusted by his soldiery as though he were prophet as well as general. As long since as the 24th March he had been engaged in the lower part of the Shenandoah Valley against General Banks, who commanded there, but had been compelled to retire to watch the proceedings of other forces entering the valley towards his rear under Fremont. The latter had been appointed to the command of Blenker's German division—the one first subtracted from M'Clellan, and notorious under its new chief for vile habits of plunder—and sent with these and some other troops to act independently of Banks in the mountains of Western Virginia. This separation of his enemies, who were again divided from a division of M'Dowall's force under Sigel, acting on the east side of the Blue Ridge, presented advantages to Jackson which his activity and daring improved to the utmost. By skilful retreats of small portions of his force (which altogether numbered under 15,000), various columns which Fremont had headed his advance with, were drawn away from their support. Their enemy then turned upon them suddenly in the hilly region on the west side of the central part of the valley, and with more active troops and better knowledge of the ground, easily concentrated a force sufficient to overwhelm them. Thus surprised on the 9th May and following days, the brigades of Generals Milroy and Schenk were utterly beaten and driven back on Franklin, a small town on the east of the main Alleghanies, through which place they had advanced. They retired thence on Fremont, who had just been sending magniloquent despatches announcing his successful advance through the mountains in pursuit of his enemy, and was now glad to pause in his advance and collect his troops in Western Virginia again.

Jackson did not follow them far. He had been informed by the country people of a sudden weakening of Banks's column by the detaching of Shields' division, ordered off by the Cabinet to strengthen M'Dowall in front of Washington; he therefore turned northward, and appeared on the 23rd May before Front Royal, where a body of Banks's troops, under Colonel Kenly, held the Manasses Gap Railroad. Their surprise was complete, and they were taken or cut to pieces, Jackson thus isolating Banks altogether from Sigel's troops about Manasses Gap Junction, as he had already separated him from Fremont. Banks advancing without delay at the news of the disaster—for though not a professional soldier, he has proved by his activity and his control of his men, an exception to the usual inefficiency of the civilian generals of the North—was encountered by the victor and driven sharply back on Winchester. A severe engagement ensued at that place on the 25th, resulting in a disastrous retreat of the Federals on Martinsburg, and so over the Potomac, abandoning the whole valley to their enemy. These brilliant operations of Jackson, by which he had delivered that country from three different forces, each about equal to his own, may bear comparison with the more famous week of victories of Napoleon in 1814; when he divided and routed corps of the Allies advancing on Paris in numbers quite overwhelming, had their generals not neglected the common-sense principles of war, and separated their armies so dangerously that they contrived to be always weakest at the point of attack.

But Jackson's success was far more than local or transitory, for it turned a doubtful struggle into one long series of triumphs for the South. Rumour, as usual, multiplied his forces, and exaggerated his projects, and the frightened Cabinet of Washington beheld him in their imagination across the Potomac, moving to attack their capital, or to isolate it from Northern support, by cutting them off from Baltimore. A paroxysm of terror followed, and the order was despatched, so fatal to M'Clellan's hopes, which not only called back M'Dowall from any attempt to join him, but enjoined the destruction of the railroad bridges between them, lest these should be used by the Southerners to strengthen Jackson.

But the Confederate Government had sounder designs in view than that of keeping a large part of their forces detached from the scene of those operations round Richmond on which the fate of the campaign really depended. They therefore ordered Jackson to move his force southward again, as quietly as might be, and to unite it to those already opposed to M'Clellan.

The latter general had now lost the hopes once existing of a speedy entrance into the southern capital. We return to his camp, and find him in an embarrassing, an almost hopeless position. His own reinforcements from the rear are few, scarce enough to supply the gaps which sickness causes in his ranks; whilst his enemy, he knows, is hourly accumulating fresh forces in his front. The Chickahominy, swollen by a season of most unusual rains, divided, as before pointed out, his army into two; and this separation made the want of bridges the more serious the farther he advanced. His extreme left was, at the end of May, within five miles of the city; but as the sole communication with the right, which had followed up the northern bank, was by the single passage near Bottom's Bridge, the position of the army has been most fitly likened to a huge V, where the two branches of the letter were really separated from any direct intercourse by a long and difficult swamp. Though by this time a number of wooden bridges had been prepared, one only was actually nearly ready for use, and that, owing to the personal caution of General Sumner, whose corps headed the right wing, and whose former attachment to the cavalry service (he had before the war commanded a regiment of dragoons) did not prevent his superintending the engineer work of his corps in person, and bringing it to a successful conclusion.

Johnson did not overlook the advantages of his situation. The news of Jackson's successes, and the panic consequent, set him free from any anxiety as to other Northern armies than that of M'Clellan. On the 21st May, therefore, he fell on the left wing of the latter, where were Keyes' corps, supported by Heintzelman's. Keyes' leading division, commanded by Casey, an old officer of the regulars, was driven, after a short resistance, a mile to the rear, with heavy loss of men, guns, and baggage. The battle was sustained, however, by Keyes, with his other division, Nagle's, which he himself led up, and, later, by

Heintzelman, whose subordinates again did good service, as at Williamsburg. The superior numbers which the Confederates had brought up did not tell at first, inasmuch as the swamps and woods for a time covered the Federal flanks effectually, and prevented their being turned. Johnson, however, was gradually towards evening pushing fresh forces down the river, and so beyond the Federal right, with the design of enveloping and destroying the whole four divisions. At this time it was that Sumner, having received orders to proceed to the assistance of the left wing, succeeded in effecting his passage of the river and swamp adjacent; and making his way direct towards the firing, debouched upon the flank of the advancing column of the enemy. With his leading division (Sedgewick's), boldly led on, he checked their progress effectually; and night put an end to the indecisive struggle, which had been begun rather late in the day for the accomplishment of any great success by the Confederates. They, however, had had good reason for their delay, as they were waiting for the swelling of the river from a flood the night before. It rose later than was expected, and Sumner had crossed his second division, under Richardson, before he was separated by it from the northern bank, where Porter, with his command of a mixed corps of volunteers and regulars, still remained. It seems to be a grave error that no attempt was made for their crossing the first day of the attack, nor any order given then; and the excuse for M'Clellan's slowness which his friends allege—that he did not feel sure till late in the day that the attack on his left was a real one—does not even, in their opinion, absolve him from reproach.

With daylight, on the 1st, the Confederates renewed their attack, but in an uncertain and desultory way; and after much skirmishing the battle died away at noon, the Northerners having recovered their original position at Seven Pines (or Fair Oaks), and inflicted a loss on the enemy—who, however, retreated unmolested—equal to, or perhaps greater than their own, which numbered 5,000. The Confederates had captured fifteen guns and considerable stores in their first advance (for Casey's division, in a not very creditable panic, had lost their whole camp-equipage, &c.); but these trophies were heavily paid for in the loss of their leader, who was severely wounded, and withdrawn from service for many months.

Lee, hitherto second in command of the army, succeeded him. A man of the same mature age, and similar high professional training, noted for extensive military knowledge and ripe judgment, he had for many years superintended * the studies of the Westpoint Academy, and was known and appreciated highly throughout the old American army. Of noble presence, great coolness in battle, and deeply devoted to the cause he had adopted—at great sacrifices, for his property in Virginia was among the first to feel the ravages of invasion—he soon won the confidence of the army. His later doings show him to be a strategist of high order, and able to carry out his conceptions to practical issue. Yet there has been an incompleteness in the results of his successes on the actual fields of strife; and we are led therefore to conclude either that Lee wants to some extent the swift *coup d'œil* and vigorous will attributed to Johnson by both friends and foes; or (which is more probably the cause), that the Confederate army is so lacking in the details of organization which make up full efficiency, as that it is easier for its chief to win victories than to reap their fruits. Their best generals feel keenly this defect of their troops, which they

* The writer visited Westpoint during the time of General Lee's charge, and saw the institution very thoroughly, passing some days there. He is able, therefore, to testify to its completeness, and the efficiency of the course of studies and discipline—never more remarkable, he believes, than at that period. General Lee, though originally an engineer, had lately, like Johnson, served in the cavalry. Such changes were not unfrequent in the U. S. army.

fully admit. The simple fact of the banishment of all strong liquors from the vicinity of Richmond, in order to assist discipline, abundantly shows how the existence of the difficulty is recognized by the Government.

The battle of Fair Oaks (or Seven Pines)—so called from the place where Casey's division was first attacked—having thus ended indecisively, and the Northern army having escaped from the immediate danger threatening them, the completion of passages over the Chickahominy at several points was pressed on and accomplished, but no other progress made during the first three weeks of June. Meanwhile the banks of the river proved fearfully unhealthy in the summer heats which followed on the rains, and M'Clellan saw his effective numbers reduced nearly a quarter by fever and dysentery, and still further by the destructive system of the volunteer regiments, under which each colonel assumed the right of granting leave to as many of his soldiers as he chose. This privilege was now most terribly abused, and the general, deprived of his originally large powers, felt himself unable to check it.*

* So little real control had M'Clellan over the discipline of his army, that in the instance of a certain volunteer regiment of cavalry, recommended by him to be disbanded as an example for disgraceful conduct before the enemy, the President decided that they should

Another division, under M'Call, had now joined him, with some further reinforcements, but the whole of them did not supply the gaps thus made in his ranks; and he might well feel uneasy as to his future when he found his fighting numbers reduced to less than 80,000, whilst the enemy were believed to be much stronger. Moreover, he required considerable detachments to guard the railroad to the Pamunkey, and the insecurity of that line of supply was strikingly demonstrated about this time by the enterprise of the Confederate cavalry under Stuart. This dashing officer, on the 14th June, led a body of his light active horse round the right of the Federals, drove off some of their cavalry whom he found near Hanover, charged the posts near White House, scattered dismay for miles among the transports on the river by firing two of them which they took, fed his troops with the choice morsels of the sutlers' shops in rear of the Northern camp, and finally recrossing the Chickahominy on the Federal left, returned safely to Richmond, having made a clear circuit of the army of M'Clellan, and caused deep

receive discharges privately, as others who had served out their time! The voice and political influence of the State Governor was raised on their behalf, and overbore the wish of the commander and the good of the whole service, which urgently called for some stern proceeding in such cases.

mortification and uneasiness to that general and his staff.*

Stuart at this time established the reputation which raised him to the chief command of the Confederate cavalry before attaining the age of thirty. But his personal fitness for important charge was well known in both armies, for he had early distinguished himself in Indian warfare when serving as lieutenant in the 1st U. S. Dragoons, the regiment of Sumner and J. Johnson.

No wonder that the Federals turned their thoughts to the James River, long since open to their gunboats to a point only a few miles from their left. The plan of transferring the whole base of operations to it was canvassed at this period: but deterred by the apparent difficulty of making the flank movement so close to the enemy, and with so very heavily encumbered an army, M'Clellan delayed the attempt until he was driven to it by defeat. Then, anxious to shield a retreat under some less painful name, he too late strove to make the "strategic movement" appear

---

* It is said that Stuart, among his other captures on this occasion, took a box addressed to General Cooke of the Federal cavalry, his own father-in-law! There were numerous instances of the division of families between the hostile camps in this extraordinary campaign. Thus the White House was first entered on the Federal advance by a nephew of Lee's, Williams of the 6th Cavalry, who had often been a guest there.

a matter of free choice, and drew on the very idea a ridicule which has been almost stamped into a proverb.

The quiescent condition of the Federals during nearly the whole of June was, of course, due to some motive for delay on both sides. M'Clellan felt his force scarce equal to maintaining their position, and his information grossly exaggerated the strength of the enemy's works. The Southern general, on his part, had determined not to make the next assault on his foe until he could do it with that overwhelming force which should finish the campaign at a blow. For this cause, covered by his intrenchments, and confining his hostile movements to a series of annoying but not serious skirmishes along the Federal front, Lee patiently awaited the expected arrival of Jackson, now on his way from the Shenandoah.

We have traced the course of successes by which that general, in the month of May, had cleared the valley from the invasions directed from each quarter; and have pointed out that, far from continuing his pursuit over the Potomac, he was intended to return southward and co-operate in the relief of Richmond. But before this movement was made, Fremont, whose advanced troops only had been repulsed, as has been seen, by Jackson, had united his forces and made another attempt to enter the valley in rear of the Confederates, whilst they were following up their successes against Banks. Jackson turned back against him, and, after some skirmishing, fell upon his enemy, who had reached the centre of the valley near Harrisonburg. A combat took place at Cross Keys, eight miles west of that little town, and Fremont's further advance was entirely checked. Shields' division had been ordered back to the valley, and attempting apparently to join Fremont, had reached Fort Republic, a small place on the Shenandoah, ten miles south-west of Harrisonburg. Leaving Cross Keys and the late disputed field, by a rapid day's march Jackson threw his forces on Shields, and drove him down the river with severe loss. He was not followed far, as Jackson was preparing to leave the valley and take all the available troops there to join Lee. He had accomplished all that was possible with his detached force; had successfully interfered to prevent M'Clellan receiving succour from the armies employed round Washington; had thus paralysed, for any effective purpose as regarded the success of the campaign, forces valued at 80,000 men; and now proceeding by the Virginia Central Railroad from Staunton through the Blue Mountains, and picking up in his course some brigades of troops which had been detached to the north of Richmond, he so effectively used his nearer communications ("acting on interior lines," in technical phrase,) as to appear at that city before any of his late adversaries knew of his departure.

It is to be noted in recounting Jackson's successes on the Shenandoah, that he had just the genius which enables a general to throw over at the right time the methodical rules of war. Thus in his advance against Banks at Winchester, he clearly left open his communications from Staunton northward to the attack of Fremont on the left and Sigel on the right. But he trusted to the difficulties which the country, and the hostile feeling of the inhabitants, with their divided commands, opposed to the junction of those generals across the valley, and judged himself capable of dealing with either singly. And for his present supplies, it must be remembered his force was small, and the country rich and favourable in its feeling. A second-rate man would have failed in such a daring movement, even if, which is most unlikely, he had had the courage to attempt it. It must also be borne in mind that Jackson evidently had the means of attaining that correct information of his opponents' movements which on their side was denied; and that the utter folly of the entire division of the invading forces gave him such an opportunity as a general but seldom meets with.

Emboldened by the long quietude of his adversaries, perhaps suspecting the non-existence of the supposed intrenchments on his front, M'Clellan, towards the end of June, began to push his left forward once more. Hooker's division, with some support, was directed, on the 25th, to take ground in advance of their position at Fair Oaks. A sharp skirmish followed, but the Confederates yielded some trifling works and a mile of ground, and M'Clellan telegraphed his last brief success on the peninsula to the Washington Cabinet. But even before the Northern journals had had time to discuss the new hope of a speedy triumph over Richmond, M'Clellan found his own safety terribly compromised, and was fain to turn all his efforts to the extrication of his army from rapidly accumulating peril. The very day of Hooker's advance he learnt of the approach of Jackson's corps, flushed with their late successes, and reported to number 80,000. Up to that very morning he had supposed Jackson fully occupied in the North! This reinforcement would turn the scale of numbers against him heavily, and he could no longer doubt why the Southerners had left him so undisturbed. He had previously had the foresight to direct some gunboats and transports to a position high up the James, about seventeen miles from his present one, in anticipation of the flank movement before referred to. Ere, however, he had finally resolved to attempt it, Lee had advanced to the attack, and the battles of the Chickahominy began.

CHAPTER IV.

RETREAT OF M'CLELLAN.

It would be as difficult as unsatisfactory to follow completely the tactical details of these conflicts, or those which followed later in the year. The same features prevail in all. Much skirmishing and noise in the woods which usually covered great part of the field—long irregular lines of infantry firing at each other across the clearings—occasionally a fierce charge of the Southerners, when they succeeded in the efforts constantly made to outflank their enemy—a strong tendency in the division and brigade commanders to act independently of any general plan; of their troops to waste their ammunition in constant volleys directed into the smoke or trees in their front—an absence of all cavalry manœuvres; partly as the small strength of that arm caused it to be husbanded, partly as the difficulties of ground prevented its action—a great deficiency in the supply of reserve ammunition, which, with the want of co-operation in the different divisions, proved fatal to continued pursuit—these make up battles long, arduous, sometimes bloody, but strikingly wanting in individual result. We must add that the democratic spirit prevailing in the Northern volunteer regiments added a great difficulty to the others weighing on their generals, for "the will of the majority" was often a will to retire at the most critical moments, and the voice of the officers, or the example of the more daring, prevailed nothing against a determination voted and carried out by the mass of the battalion. The battle of Gaines' Hill only is entered into at length as a striking instance of what is here asserted of many such combats.

To return to actual events. The general plan of the Confederate commander was to throw the weight of his attack on M'Clellan's right, and, if successful, to extend his own left, so as to seize the line of the railroad, cut the Federals off from White House, and finally drive them off to the south, where a large morass, called White Oak Swamp, lay between them and the James River. To prevent their passing through this in any order, or carrying off their stores, a large force would remain in front of Richmond to interfere with any attempt of M'Clellan's to make an orderly flank movement by the passages through the

RETREAT OF M'CLELLAN. 61

swamp. The complete success of this plan seemed to imply little short of destruction or surrender of the Federal forces; but the latter part, it will be seen, was not carried out, and it is probable that Lee reckoned too much on his superiority of force (he had about 90,000 available troops, Jackson's included, and M'Clellan not over 80,000), and divided his army over too large a circle, in his effort to envelope his enemy entirely.

Jackson being now close at hand, the attack of the Confederates began on the afternoon of the 26th. General D. Hill led 20,000 men over the Chickahominy, and advanced against the Federal right, now consisting of Porter's three divisions only. Of these, M'Call's was advanced about a mile from the river to a place called Mechanicsville, and upon him fell the brunt of the first day's fighting. However, the position being good, and intrenched beforehand, the Confederates made little progress. Porter's second division, under Morell, prevented their turning M'Call by any movement in his rear along the river, and the day closed, after long skirmishing, and considerable loss to the Northerners from the concentrated fire of a very superior number of the enemy's guns, without much advantage to either side.

In the night, however, Jackson was arriving from

Hanover Courthouse, near which he left the railroad, and moving his troops to Hill's left, to join in a renewed attack next day. On his part, M'Clellan abandoned the hope of maintaining his communications with York River, and resolved to escape for the present to the James, where the gunboats might restore the equality of force, and his supplies be uninterrupted. Orders had already been given for the commencement of the necessary movement, and the train was to move on night and day, there being only one road for the carriages, and that much exposed to flank attack from the direction of Richmond. Stoneman, with the cavalry, was detached towards White House, to break up the depôt there, and destroy what could not be removed. To Porter was entrusted the covering of the bridges of the Chickahominy, lately constructed with so much pains. His corps comprised two divisions of volunteers, as before noticed, and that of Sykes, the former reserve of regular troops; it was supported by two regiments of cavalry.

Early on the 27th, M'Call's division retired five miles down the river, and took up the position of Gaines' Hill, on the ground where Porter had his other troops arranged, and partly intrenched in front of the bridges to be protected. This latter general, a man of heavy reserved manner, and not over popular in the army, justified M'Clellan's selection of him for the post of honour, by the obstinacy with which he received the attacks directed against him the whole morning by Hill and Jackson, who were joined by Longstreet. The fight grew hotter and hotter. Porter called loudly for reinforcements, and the incessant sound of artillery on his side showed M'Clellan that the Confederates were really throwing their strength there. He, till late in the day, had feared that an attack, really false, from the Richmond direction, might be pressed against his left wing, so as to call for all his reserves. Now, however, he ordered Slocum's and Richardson's divisions to be successively passed over to the north bank. The bridge, or series of bridges, to be traversed was several hundred yards long, and the operation slow. Before the reinforcements had made their way over, the troops of Porter, stricken by some causeless panic, had almost entirely abandoned their position.

The manner of the thing was this. Alarmed probably by the near approach of the firing in their front to the sole means of retreat, some of the troops in the rear began to fall back towards the bridges—not flying indeed—but marching coolly off their ground. First they moved by twos and threes; then by sections: finally, companies, officers and all, faced about and moved rearwards, disregarding wholly the threats and entreaties of their commanders. "We're tired out fighting;" "Got no more ammunition;" "Guess the rebels will be down to them bridges soon;" were their only replies to the expostulations of the indignant staff who strove to turn them. The French princes serving with M'Clellan here particularly * exerted themselves, but in vain. Porter himself was fairly overcome by the torrent, and seemed to feel the uselessness of further contending against it. The panic went on from rear to front, affecting even the regulars of Sykes; and the regiments who were near the enemy began naturally enough to follow the example of their supports. The 6th Cavalry, and Rush's Lancers, a volunteer regiment, were ordered up to check the advancing foe, but their advance ended in a few pistol shots, and a retreat which added to the panic of the infantry, who mistook them for a pursuing body of Confederate horse. The gunners of the batteries now in turn deserted their charge, and nothing saved the Federals from a terrible disaster, but the fact that the full extent of their dissolution was greatly concealed from the enemy by the quantity of wood which covered the front, and that the Confederates—as usual in the

* The writer has this matter from a disinterested witness.

afternoon of their battles—had exhausted their ammunition.

Richardson's and Slocum's troops, however, now appeared, boldly led on by their respective brigadiers. French, and Meagher with his Irishmen, here specially distinguished themselves by the rapidity of their march and their readiness to take share in the fight. They did not, indeed — as represented in Federal accounts—rush with the bayonet at the foe; but they deployed their brigades, covered the retreating divisions with their skirmishers, and checked the Confederate troops on their advance. These were not only short of ammunition, but wearied with marching and fighting for two long days; and they allowed the coming darkness to close on the field without pursuing their success further. Considerable it was indeed already, for they had 4,000 prisoners, wounded and unwounded, in their hands, and twenty-five of Porter's guns had been totally abandoned in the rout, and gave substantial proof of his defeat.

There were about 36,000 men engaged on the Federal side this day at Gaines' Hill, and much skirmishing took place in the false attack round Hooker's posts on their left. The Confederates are believed to have had nearly 50,000 troops on the north bank of the river, for large reserves were moved up, under Longstreet and other generals, during the early part of the fight: many of these, however, were too wearied to be engaged.

M'Clellan had not decided on the march to the James without considering other courses. It seemed, however, every way preferable to a retreat on the Pamunkey, in a direction already flanked by Jackson. To remain on the defensive wholly was clearly out of the question, now that the bridges to the north bank were already near capture. Seriously the Federal chief revolved the possibility of a sudden concentration, and a direct move on Richmond; and the works between his left and the city, it is since ascertained, were hardly capable of effective resistance to a sudden general attack. But then the question arose, what would become of the Northern army shut up in Richmond, and with every approach for reinforcements closed; and the idea was abandoned as overbold. Probably, the movement on Turkey Creek was, after all, the least critical that could have been attempted in the face of Lee's 90,000 troops.

Before daylight on the 28th, the troops were drawn to the south bank, and the bridges broken. The enemy continued their movement along the north bank, and soon possessed themselves of the crossing of the railway and river close to Savage's station, thus dividing the retreating army from all property abandoned on the line to White House. The skirmishes this day were insignificant, but M'Clellan found his rearguard's situation so precarious, that he was compelled to draw it in at the cost of abandoning his field hospitals with 1,300 wounded in them.

On the 29th, Jackson attempted to drive in General Sumner's troops, who were covering the passage of the waggons from the camps near Savage's station, but the Federals, aided by the exceeding difficulties of the ground—a mixture of wood and swamp—held their own tolerably. On their left, near Fair Oaks, the fighting was still more severe, for M'Clellan had abandoned his intrenchments there in order to place his troops in a more concentrated position, which should cover the passage leading from Richmond into the White Oak Swamp. Encouraged by this apparent retreat, the Confederates advanced somewhat rashly upon the position which Heintzelman's two divisions, aided by Sedgewick's, occupied under protection of a very heavy artillery. The fire of this latter, and the good behaviour of Heintzelman's corps under their excellent leaders, obtained a temporary success in this affair, which the Northerners call the battle of Peach Orchard. On this same day, detachments of cavalry from the Confederate left occupied

White House, and captured such stores (and the amount according to Southern accounts was considerable) as had not been removed or destroyed; but great part had been run into the river in railroad cars, and so sunk.*

M'Clellan had taken no personal share in the fighting, feeling evidently that his first duty was the superintendence of the march of his baggage-encumbered troops on their toilsome movement, and affording us plain proof how sadly his army lacked that proper care and ordering which is entrusted in those of Europe to the staff, so as to leave the general-in-chief free for the larger duties of his station. His patience and fortitude, his calm, unruffled temper amid accumulating vexations, won the admiration of all near him, and gave confidence to his disheartened troops. These qualities were so shown on this occasion as to chain to him the affections of the army to an extent hereafter to exercise much influence on the conduct of the war; they had their present reward when he knew that evening that his leading columns, under Keyes and Porter (the latter's troops had been purposely sent on, as it was feared their *morale* was shaken by their severe

---

* The house itself was fired this day—accidentally, according to Northern accounts.

handling on the 27th), had cleared the swamp, and reached the gunboats on the James at the destined point near Turkey Creek.

On the 30th, the Confederates saw that their enemy was slipping out of their grasp, and made fierce attacks on his left and rear. Sumner commanded the troops (chiefly Franklin's men) still on the march from Savage's station, and though closely pressed by Jackson, the stout old veteran used the advantages of the difficult ground on either side the road so well, that the enemy gained no serious trophies from his divisions. Meanwhile Hill and Longstreet, leaving Jackson to conduct the immediate pursuit, directed their course along the Chickahominy, and crossed that river lower down at Long Bridge, moving towards a village on the James, called Charles City, below the point which M'Clellan made for; but the distance they had to traverse was so considerable that they never seriously outflanked him. A more dangerous move was that attempted by Lee's orders along the road leading from Richmond down the left bank of the James. Magruder headed the Confederates here, and soon came into collision with Heintzelman, who was charged with the defence of the approach from that side, and had his own two divisions and M'Call's under his orders. So furious was the onset that the latter was completely broken, its general wounded and taken, fifteen guns captured, and the safety of the column under Sumner, still entangled in the swamp, seriously threatened. But Heintzelman's men retreated coolly, and the pursuers coming suddenly within range of the *Galena,* and other heavily armed gunboats, these opened on the Confederates a heavy and sustained fire of their huge shells. Owing to the dense wood all around, the damage done was but trifling; but the noise created by the crashing of these great projectiles through the trees was so terrific that it staggered the Confederates, and produced among them so much panic that Heintzelman made an advance, and recovered the ground he had lost. The movement of the main column of the Northerners upon their new position was then completed successfully. Porter's troops covered the right front of the new line, which was at a place called Malvern Hill, and the Confederates making a loose attack upon him just before dark, were driven off by the artillery fire.

M'Clellan, not expecting to remain unmolested in his present attitude, prepared skilfully to receive the attack of the enemy. His left was completely covered by the gunboats. The ground in front of his army, much narrowed by the vicinity of Turkey Creek, sloped away gently, and being open, was perfectly swept by the fire of his batteries, nearly 300 guns being disposed for this purpose. To his right the approach was more difficult, and some rude intrenchments of felled trees were easily created to strengthen this flank effectually.

Nothwithstanding these difficulties the Confederates on the morning of the 1st July, indignant at the escape of their enemy from the net they had thrown round him, advanced to the attack. Heintzelman, who had passed the night four miles higher up the river in order to cover some straggling portions of the convoy, delayed by the darkness on the road from Savage's station, which intersected that direct from Richmond at a point in his rear just in front of Turkey Creek, saw his charge safely over the latter. He then followed them over the bridge and fell back on Malvern Hill to occupy the centre of the position, as had been arranged. To the left were Keyes' troops, and the relics of Sumner's and Porter's on the right. The whole front was about a mile and a half long, and much of this under the fire of the iron-clads in the river. At about four P.M. the Confederates made a general attack; but it perfectly failed against the overwhelming fire opposed to them, and after continuing it until they proved this by a useless carnage of 2,000 of their number (owing much, it was said, to the violence of their leading general, Magruder, who was charged with having lost his temper and head), they were drawn off, leaving the Federals to claim a success, which somewhat cheered them at the end of their long and harassing retreat. Magruder paid the penalty of this ill close of the six days' triumphal Confederate pursuit, by a suspension from his command, a punishment which seems harsh, when we consider his previous services in April in checking M'Clellan's first advance with his small force. His admirable firmness at Yorktown shows him plainly a man of great character and courage; and his skill as an artillerist, acquired in the service of the old United States army, was conspicuously shown in his defence of the lines there entrusted to his charge with a very inadequate garrison. He has been since restored to service, and employed in Texas, where he has again distinguished himself for energy and boldness.

The contest over, M'Clellan moved at nightfall seven miles down the James to a place called Harrison's Landing, where he had not only a secure position, but a better approach for his transports, some of which had already come round with their supplies, and were considerably exposed to annoyance in the narrow winding part of the river near Turkey Creek. The lesson at Malvern Hill had taught the Confederates to respect him with his new supports, the iron-clads; and he was attacked no more. His army, much exhausted on their arrival at the James, soon gathered strength and spirits, and, with undiminished confidence in their chief, looked forward to a resumption of their advance against the city. But he felt himself too weak to resume the offensive. The losses on the retreat (26th June to 1st July inclusive) were officially reported at 17,500, and he was left with scarce 60,000 fighting men, facing a victorious opponent, who had, before his successful advance, the larger army; and whose numbers had not shrunk so much on the whole, despite the disadvantages of attacking intrenchments—for the Federals owned to having left from 7,000 to 8,000 prisoners in the enemy's hands. The latter claimed also to have captured 63 guns and immense quantities of stores.

Here we may leave M'Clellan for a while. His peninsular campaign may now be considered as closed. No official versions of the details of "the strategic movement" to the James could hide the one great fact that the Army of the Potomac had been checked and repulsed with terrible loss of men, *matériel,* and reputation. For a time the wildest rumours of evil had currency, and it was expected that the whole of the Federal troops would lay down their arms at the summons of Lee; and when these rumours had died away, and the actual state of things became known, the clamour against the unfortunate general did not die with them. The same press which had rated him as "the young Napoleon," now had no language strong enough to condemn him with. As the worthy Sumner, whose personal activity and energy had turned the battle of Fair Oaks, was then abused for not having arrived earlier in the field, and won a decisive victory; so M'Clellan was now blamed for the huge losses of the retreat, which his conduct had prevented being turned into an utterly ruinous flight. Bitterly did he now reap the fruit of his submitting to have his arrangements and plans thwarted, as they had from the first been, by his jealous chief, the War Secretary Stanton. And when he urged on the Washington Cabinet the feasibility of the attack of Richmond, by the way of the James, he found his suggestions wholly disregarded. He was refused reinforcements, and had only to hold his own until he should be removed from the peninsula altogether.

Nor can his conduct wholly escape criticism. The

over-caution which marked it throughout is owned by some of his best friends as a real fault. Especially it must be remarked that, after the battle of Fair Oaks and the completion of his bridges, he threw away a reasonable chance of advancing against Richmond, when the defending army was much less numerous than his own. He was deterred probably by supposed intrenchments in his front, which existed only in rumour; or, at least, were greatly exaggerated as to their strength, as before remarked. There were no works of any great importance existing, save the redoubts close to the city. It should be remembered in thus judging, that the attempt to proceed by direct attack upon the enemy's capital, would necessarily have been desperately resisted, and, if not completely successful, would have placed the assailants in a most critical position.

CHAPTER V.

POPE'S CAMPAIGN IN VIRGINIA.

A NEW military light now appeared at Washington. General Halleck, hitherto directing the operations in the West, though taking no personal share in them, was called to the chief command of the armies of the North, which the President had nominally exercised since M'Clellan's deposition. Known to be a diligent student of theoretical strategy, he had not enhanced his reputation by the conduct of the campaign in Tennessee, which, beginning with great successes, had come to an inglorious end at Pittsburg. But the Government had evidently ascribed the near destruction of Grant's army on that occasion to the carelessness of the immediate commander, and now, hard driven for some one of name enough to be made their responsible military adviser, they called Halleck from the Mississippi to their aid. On the 11th July, the order appeared which gave him the control of the land forces of the Union; and it was understood his first care was to be directed to the withdrawal of M'Clellan's army from its doubtful position on the James.

Already the Government, on the first news of the Chickahominy disaster, had issued orders for a further levy of volunteers; the numbers in each State to be filled up *by impressment,* if necessary; but without waiting for their formation, it was resolved to attempt an advance against Richmond on the Alexdria and Orange line, with a view to divert the attention of the Confederates from the Army of the Potomac—as that at Harrison's Landing was still designated. This new expedition was entrusted to General Pope, who had been named in June to the chief control of the corps under Fremont, Banks, and M'Dowall; when Jackson's brilliant successes had taught the Federals practically the danger of divided commands and separate lines of operation.

Pope was junior on the list of generals to those whom he thus superseded. Formerly employed in the Mexican War, he had seen service as captain of infantry. Brought early in the year into a small command in the combined expedition directed down the Mississippi, he had made a considerable name at the capture of New Madrid and the intrenched Island

No. 10. The striking success of the Federals at the latter was ascribed to his talent and activity. Transferred to the army opposed to Beauregard while the latter held Corinth, he had charge of the advanced guard which followed the Confederates on their retreat from that position, and had claimed great successes in the pursuit; but the faith of his admirers was somewhat shaken when the 10,000 prisoners he declared he had taken were reduced to 100 in the more simple narrative of the Southern general. Perhaps it was in reference to this difference of estimate that the President, who personally selected him for his present appointment, gave him the doubtful praise of combining "great talents, great indolence, and great want of veracity." Certain it is, he had already acquired in the army the reputation of a braggart; although his friends asserted his claims to boldness and activity, such as should bring a new phase into the Northern war.

It may be that Pope's sudden elevation somewhat upset his judgment. For on his arrival at Washington he impressed many who saw him with the idea that his dark piercing eye and quick manner betokened great energy and power; and the popular voice was, in consequence, as ready to flatter him into a belief of his own invincibility, as it had been to adore M'Clellan not long before for his self-guarded reticence. But Pope was more ready than the latter to look for such flattery; and, as though to stamp himself at once as "the coming man" of his day, he announced ostentatiously his intent to conduct the war upon new and improved principles. "He had heard much," he said, "of lines of communication and lines of retreat. The only line a general should know anything of, in his opinion, was *the line of his enemy's retreat.*" His treatment of the recusant inhabitants of East Virginia should be also, he gave out, something quite different from that which M'Clellan had used. He would civilize that district much in the same manner as Cromwell is said to have made Ulster Protestant, by expatriating all his enemies. All citizens within the lines of Pope's army, as it advanced, were to take the oath of allegiance, or to be banished south: perjury or exile was the choice of the happy Virginians, wherever subjected to this new and vigorous government.

Such proofs of zeal and genius as these, publicly announced in Pope's general orders on assuming command, led his admirers to anticipate great events from his action. His orders were to advance on the line of the Orange railroad, if not as far as Richmond—for which his means might be inadequate—

yet at least to the point of Gordonsville, where the Virginia central line is met. The occupation of this place would so paralyse the chief communications of Richmond with the west, as at once to draw the enemy's attention in that direction, and leave M'Clellan free to embark from the peninsula, without the danger of being attacked during the operation.

Pope's troops were pushed onwards in the first part of July, with no other delay than that necessary to form along the railroad the large depôts which their wants required. These, however, caused much encumbrance; for though the troops did not carry with them, as some of M'Clellan's force had in their transports, whole sets of household furniture, yet they had far more to convey than the most luxuriously fitted European army ever requires. It was evident from the very beginning that anything like a sudden retreat would involve not merely much sacrifice of baggage, but also unwonted confusion and difficulty. However, for a time matters went smoothly, no enemy being visible. Towards the middle of July, the general, announcing to all inquirers that henceforth his head-quarters " would be in the saddle," left Alexandria in a special train decked out with flags and branches in honour of the triumphs to be won by his new force, the " Army of Virginia."

Fremont having resigned his command upon being superseded, was succeeded by Sigel, an exiled leader of the Revolutionary party, who had fought in Western Germany in 1849. He had been early entrusted with a division, as bearing a name well known to the German emigrants, and specially likely to attach those of the hotter sort to the Federal colours. Under Pope's orders were, therefore, at present the corps of Banks, Sigel, and M'Dowall, to which others from the army of the Potomac were to be added, when they could be brought from the peninsula. His cavalry were few and bad, and though not equal to the needful outpost and advance duties, they were further employed and wearied out in the task of enforcing the oath of allegiance in the scattered population, in order that the Northern press might gloat over the scenes arising from this driving in of the Secessionist farmers at the lance's point to forswear themselves. No open enemy, however, appeared as yet. The head-quarters of the army passed in succession Bull's Run and the Rappahannock, and reached the Rapidan, the southern fork of the latter stream; pushing the cavalry on to Orange Courthouse, a point on the railroad near Gordonsville. This latter place the advanced guard came within six miles of upon the 18th July, when they were driven back by detachments of Confederate horse. Pope now was preparing to move in force in the latter place, when, about the 5th August, he became aware of considerable forces advancing against him, and fearing to involve himself with the mass of the army of Lee, retired a few miles and kept his front behind and at some distance from the Rapidan, waiting to discover the strength of the enemy. The latter proved to be the ubiquitous corps of Jackson, who had been detached from Richmond to check Pope's further advance. He, finding the corps of the latter occupying a very extended front, moved a small part of his force over the Rapidan far to his left, in order to keep them divided, for he had with him scarce half the number of the Federals, and yet he purposed, according to his former tactics, assuming the offensive. Pope was at first deceived, and expected the attack on his right where Sigel lay watching the roads near Madison; but on the 8th inclined to the belief that it would be made on the main road from Orange to Culpepper, and drew in his corps towards the latter place, which was his own head-quarters, advancing Banks in the direction of the Rapidan. On the 9th, Banks continued his movement slowly, supported by M'Dowall; but Jackson's force had now crossed the river, and were occupying in strength a woody hill called Cedar Mountain; they were soon seen posted on the north side of it, which sloped away gently into corn-fields surrounding it in the direction of the Federal advance. Banks had no orders to attack, but having thrown out skirmishers, they soon became engaged with those of the enemy, and the former followed them up with his supports, till a general attack was made on the Confederate leader's position, just as he desired. He had prepared his batteries skilfully to receive it. After an hour's engagement he drove back the Federals with ease from his front, and advancing his left suddenly on them through the corn, surprised and broke a brigade under General Prince, who was taken, with several hundreds of his men. The engagement did not begin until 6 P.M., and was soon ended by the darkness; but Pope, though he arrived before that time, incautiously allowed Banks' troops to bivouac within range of the enemy's position. About midnight the latter, having observed this mistake, suddenly opened a heavy fire upon the weary Northerners, causing great loss, and a terrible panic which carried many of them miles to the rear, into Culpepper itself.

Jackson forwarded his prisoners at once to Richmond, where the officers were kept in durance, and held ready, under a retaliatory proclamation of President Davis, issued in consequence of Pope's threats against the country people, to answer with their lives for any ill-treatment of the latter by the Northern army.* It was not his "strategy" with a single corps to face Pope in the open country, when he expected soon the arrival of Lee's main army. He therefore sent a flag of truce to arrange with the enemy to bury their own dead. This circumstance, and the fact that Jackson, two days later, retired over the Rapidan again—confident that he had checked his opponent sufficiently by the combat of Cedar Mountain, yet anxious to detain him as long as possible in his present advanced position—induced Pope to represent his repulse to his superiors at Washington as a success! He remained some time confronting the Confederates on the Rapidan; but on the 17th August fell back, and crossed the Rappahannock, for he had heard that Lee himself had arrived in his front.

That general had now abandoned the idea of any further attack on M'Clellan, and had been preparing to follow Jackson to the North with all available

---

* This retaliation was never enforced, owing to Pope's speedy removal from the command of the army of Virginia.

forces. By the 5th August, the army of the Potomac had discovered that the enemy were no longer near them in any considerable strength; and Hooker's division, having advanced as far as the old battle-ground of Malvern Hill, had driven back a small body of the Confederates left there in observation. But nothing came of the skirmish, and M'Clellan could only carry out the positive orders of his superior, under which, by a rapid and well-arranged movement, he marched his army through Williamsburg to Yorktown without molestation, and thence conveyed them by water to Washington. The last of them reached that city about the 20th August, and as the corps landed they were considered as liable to be detached from M'Clellan's command; and they were actually despatched in succession to reinforce Pope; Heintzelman being first sent, then Porter, and, much later, Sumner and Franklin; Keyes retiring from service for a time. M'Clellan, meanwhile, remained in charge of the forces at Alexandria—whither many of the newly-raised volunteer regiments were hastening—until the end of August.

Pope remained for some days after his retreat over the Rappahannock guarding the fords of that river, whilst Lee was collecting his army on the southern bank. The Confederates had now nearly 70,000 men in their new line. Hitherto the arrangement of their forces had been entirely by divisions, except for temporary purposes; but they considered the time now arrived for enhancing the usefulness of the chief lieutenants of Lee, and improving the organization, by forming *corps d'armée*. The Virginian army was therefore now chiefly divided into two corps: Jackson's, soon to become famous as the division he had led before; and another of greater strength under Longstreet, a general whose ability and perfect soldierly bearing had been raising him in estimation ever since he was first distinguished at Bull's Run. To these corps was added a reserve under General D. Hill; and some unattached brigades were moving up in rear of all. Pope had less than 50,000, and was looking anxiously for Heintzelman and Porter, who were bringing him each 10,000 men from Alexandria. Some unimportant skirmishing took place during the week that thus passed, but the river was high, and the attempts of Lee to surprise a passage were probably but feints to occupy his enemy, whilst Jackson's corps was secretly moved up the river considerably to the left of the main army, for a separate and decisive operation.

On the 22nd, the Federal commander narrowly escaped capture by one of the dashing "raids" for which Stuart has become so famous. This latter officer, crossing the river at some unguarded passage on the Federal right with about a thousand horse, and guided, doubtless, by some of the inhabitants whom Pope had lately been employed in converting to Unionism, rode straight to that general's head-quarters, which were at Catlett's, a small railroad station, twelve miles from the river. The guard of four companies of rifles dispersed with the utmost celerity, but Pope and most of his staff escaped, having not long before ridden to the front on a reconnaissance. Stuart captured, however, a number of prisoners, and took the whole of the personal baggage and official papers of the Federal general, bringing all back to the Confederate lines in triumph, without losing a man. This exploit was only the prelude to another movement of the same nature, made on so large a scale as to be decisive of the result of the campaign, by Jackson and his fleet corps, known, from their well-proved marching powers, as the " foot cavalry " of the South.

We have said that that corps, which consisted of three divisions, of about 6,000 men each, had been moved gradually, and without the knowledge of the Federals, to the extreme left of Lee's army, and high up the Rappahannock. On the 25th they commenced the operation of moving completely round Pope's right by a march directed first up to the sources of the river, then along the eastern slope of the Blue Ridge, through a farming country of quiet settlers, which neither of the contending armies had yet reached. Impeded by no carriages but those of the needful reserve of ammunition, and the guns attached to the divisions, living on the corn which grew along their path, and such other small supplies as the sympathizing country-people offered, they wound their way past the little town of Orleans, through a mountain district called Fauquier, and so on over a highly elevated tract between the Blue and Bull's Run mountains, reaching the Manasses Gap Railroad at night, at a station in the hills called Salem. The next day saw them following the line through Thoroughfare Gap, and then striking slightly to their right they descended through the little town of Gainsville, and came upon the Orange Railroad at Bristow Station, having accomplished a march of forty-five miles in the two days. At Bristow they came at once upon trains laden with supplies for Pope, which were seized, and plundered or destroyed. They had repeated, indeed, the manœuvre Napoleon had practised on various occasions in his earlier campaigns, of throwing himself upon the well-furnished line of supply of his adversaries, trusting the support of his troops to what they could take for themselves.

General Pope, in his report of these events, declares that he knew the movement that was being made, and that he trusted the defence of his depôts near Manasses Junction to a division expected from Alexandria, though he does not explain how this division was to meet and repulse *the* 25,000 *troops* for which he gives Jackson credit in the same despatch. Be that as it may, on the 27th he learnt certainly that the railroad in his rear was completely in his enemy's possession. He took his resolution at once with a promptness which does him credit, and shows him to be by no means so destitute of the elements of military science as his own words had before made him appear. Porter and Heintzelman having arrived, his forces numbered nearly 60,000; yet he felt that he was not equal to the task of breaking through the enemy in rear, and keeping at bay Lee and the unknown force which confronted him on the Rappahannock. He did, therefore, the only thing which remained to be done, and, turning his face towards Washington, directed a general movement of his whole army in that direction, in order to force Jackson out of the path before Lee could follow him and take share in the fight.

His march was in three columns. M'Dowall moved from Warrenton along the turnpike-road on Gainsville, forming a left wing with his own corps and Sigel's. Pope himself moved on the right along the railroad with Banks' troops, part of Heintzelman's, and Porter's. General Reno, who had brought a single division to the army, marched with it and Kearney's (the second division of Heintzelman's) by a country road between the two. This movement was begun on the 27th.

That morning Jackson, having finished his work at Bristow, marched along the railroad on Manasses Gap Junction to seize the depôts there. This was successfully done, and a brigade under General Taylor, which had been sent from Alexandria upon the report of some Confederates being seen near the Junction, was dispersed with much loss to the Federals by a sudden attack, in which their leader was mortally wounded. Public stores and private luxuries to an immense amount here fell into Jackson's hands, and his soldiers were enabled to repay themselves for the privations of their march by a feast at their enemies' expense. This was not enjoyed in quietude, however, for Ewell's division, the last to move from Bristow, was by this time engaged with the advance of Pope under Hooker, and a sharp skirmish ensued as the

Confederates moved onwards to join the main body. Night put a stop to this, and the darkness was lighted up soon after by the conflagration of the storehouses and railroad waggons accumulated at the Junction. These destroyed, Jackson moved northward and crossed Bull's Run, avoiding as long as possible an action with Pope, for he felt the critical nature of his position, between the trebly superior forces of the latter and the mass of troops at Alexandria. Mere hardihood, without prudence, might have exposed his corps to the fate of the unhappy one commanded by Vandamme in 1813 at Culm, which was destroyed in an unsupported attempt to arrest the retreat of the allies from Dresden, by a movement upon their rear of the same nature as that just performed by the Confederate general. Indeed, M'Dowall was following him up closely by the Warrenton Road, and threatened to come between him and the Gap of Manasses, so as to cut him off from succour. Another severe skirmish closed this day between the advance of the left Federal column and the right of Jackson's line, which was held successfully on the defensive in a strong position close to that road.

On the morning of the 29th, Jackson had his three divisions drawn up very nearly on the same ground which M'Dowall had covered in his advance against the Confederates on the morning of the first battle of Bull's Run. The left was near Centreville, under Ewell; the centre was Jackson's old division, still under his personal command; the right extended behind the stream in the direction of the Gap. Upon this division, under General A. Hill, fell the brunt of a very severe day's fighting. Jackson was aware that Longstreet was marching to his assistance, and obstinately held his position, which flanked the road along which Pope's troops would move to obtain clear passage towards Alexandria, and yet enabled him to unite with the Confederate succours coming through the Gap. Pope strove to overwhelm his opponent before fresh forces could arrive, and drive him back upon the mountains, as well to obtain the *éclat* of a success as to clear his own passage; for, although his troops had entered Centreville the night before, and so come into communication with the succours arriving from Alexandria, the enemy were still unpleasantly near the road leading to the former place from Warrenton.

Heintzelman moved against Jackson's left, and Sigel his centre, whilst M'Dowall was ordered with Porter to attempt to turn the right of the position. This latter movement was not carried out however, for Porter either could not, or would not, perform the part assigned to him of flanking Hill's troops (he has since been deprived of his commission for his conduct on this occasion), and Pope, in his report, attributed the small result of the day's fighting to his disobedience. After many desultory attacks, Jackson yielded ground slightly, inflicting terrible loss on the Federal divisions that pressed his front, and Pope telegraphed a victory to Washington. But towards evening, a division of his army, under Ricketts, who had been posted the day before to attempt to guard the approach from Thoroughfare Gap, fell back on Porter, under whom they were placed, and opened the way altogether to the advance of Longstreet, who emerged from the hills, and brought his troops out on Jackson's right, having followed the same route to the Junction as the latter general.

The Federal troops had exhausted most of their ammunition and supplies, and there had been no proper concert of their chief with M'Clellan at Alexandria for the furnishing of either, to enable them to continue the struggle. They were wearied and disheartened in the extreme, and the division generals had no confidence in their chief; some of them, clearly Porter for one, having little mind to obey or sustain him. In short, the army generally felt the depressing effects of a retreat conducted under a leader whom they had seen outmanœuvred, and the Confederate forces arriving were enormously magnified by camp rumour, so that D. Hill and Longstreet were reported to be about to lead 200,000 troops to outflank and cut them off from Alexandria! The Confederates, on the other hand, were full of spirit and ardour, and Jackson's three divisions, the only ones yet seriously engaged, had replenished their cartouche-boxes from the spoils of their enemies' depôt, and were burning to renew the contest with the support of the newly arrived reinforcements, which they felt assured them victory.

The Archduke Charles, in his great work on strategy, points out that there are a certain class of battles which, being led to by successful strategetic movements, are won, in fact, before they are fought. Of these the second battle of Bull's Run was one. Lee had now arrived and assumed command, and on the morning of the 30th began the attack by skirmishing, so as to cover the continued advance of Longstreet, whose corps, pivoting by its left on Jackson's right, was gradually wheeled up, and in the afternoon occupied a line nearly perpendicular to his, and flanking the Federal left. The battle commenced in earnest at about 1 P.M., but from the first the army of Pope gave ground, and suffered terribly under the concentrated fire brought on them, especially against Porter's corps, which formed the left this day. Fortunately for their escape, the proceedings of the previous day had ended in their passing Jackson so far that, though part of their line was still in Centreville, they now looked from that place westward towards the ground about the stream, and had their rear on the road to Fairfax and Alexandria. At night they had fallen back completely to the rising ground about Centreville, where a few faithful troops had stood to cover the disgraceful flight from the battle in 1861. Franklin, with his corps of two weak divisions, now arrived, and Sumner was close behind him. They brought with them 20,000 men; but this number only repaired the losses sustained in the previous week — according to Pope's own account—and none of the generals, except Sumner whose stout heart struggled against retreat, desired to face the victorious foe. Yet the latter also showed evident exhaustion; for the 31st passed by without any further direct attempt of Lee to press his advantage.

The next day that general, though not moving on Centreville, was discovered to be advancing Jackson's corps to his left through the hills, in order to force

Pope to continue his retreat, at the risk of being flanked. This contingency the Federal general would not face, and retired through Fairfax, without attempting more than the usual defence of rearguard positions. But Lee had already gained somewhat on him; and although the troops from the Potomac army behaved well, considering the series of disasters they had gone through, a good deal of confusion occurred when Jackson's approach to the road beyond Fairfax was seen by the Federals. In attempting to restore order and courage, two of the best of the Federal generals fell, Stevens and Kearney. The latter has been already mentioned, and deserves special notice indeed, as one of the most ardent soldiers of his time, who here ended, prematurely, a career which had already embraced, before the civil war called him again to the field, campaign service in three of the four quarters of the world.

The retreat continued, and after some further skirmishing, the next day, the 2nd September, saw the last of the discomfited host dragging its weary way into the welcome shelter of the Alexandria lines. Well then was the foresight justified which had caused M'Clellan to expend so much time and labour on these the previous autumn. But for their protecting front we may well imagine how easily the army of

Lee would have entered Washington, and how terrible a blow the Northern prestige of strength would have suffered. But this calamity Halleck and Stanton escaped by the prudence of the man whom they had ill-used first, and since have striven, by every possible means, to vilify; for Lee understood his craft too well to throw his men's lives away in open assaults on heavily-armed works, manned by an army at least equal to his own in number.

Meanwhile, as the thunder of the Southern guns drew near, terror and distraction ruled in the Cabinet of Washington. The President and his advisers could not conceal from themselves that their chosen general had proved a lamentable failure, and his recent mendacious claims to victory now rendered the reality of defeat more painful and startling. Looking round for some one to bring order out of the chaos of beaten troops and undrilled levies who were meeting round the capital, their eyes fell naturally on the man who had once before organized for them an army, which at least seemed capable of great things. M'Clellan's command had, as has been shown, been taken bit by bit from him; and he had been left at one time in charge of only a few hundred men, and the works they watched. Nay, it had been intended to put him aside altogether, and Pope's success would have been the signal for his dismissal from employ. But now it was seen clearly that to him the soldiers looked as the only one man who could retrieve their misfortune. The attachment of his old army clung to him so strongly as to affect all around, and so necessary did his re-appointment to chief command become, under the urgent pressure of the moment, that, had he been possessed with a more selfish spirit, he might have stipulated for any terms he pleased. But he accepted the trust as soon as offered,* and was placed at the head of all the forces round Washington, with such general permission to use his own means for covering and defending the city, as was implied by the absence of all definite instructions. He assumed command on the 2nd September, in consequence of a vague verbal request given through General Halleck; and finding that, owing to the jealousy and timidity of the Cabinet, his proper official appointment to the conduct of the new campaign was delayed indefinitely, he took upon himself

* One thing he required in assuming the command was the release of General Stone, unjustly imprisoned and kept without trial ever since the affair of Ball's Bluff in the previous autumn. But Stanton's animosity against that unhappy man burnt still strongly, and M'Clellan preferred giving up the point for the time, rather than risking the safety of the State by an open rupture with the Government. For a similar reason, he took with him Hooker and other officers who had shown personal jealousy and ill-feeling towards himself.

the responsibility of acting without it. No doubt, he felt that the terror inspired by the Confederate approach would, for the present, preserve him from the interference of Lincoln and Stanton. This was indeed the case; and for a short time he wielded (strange spectacle in a free nation!) the full powers of a generalissimo, without any authority but that derived from the imbecility of the Government and the confidence of the troops. Before he had time to arrange the confused mass put under him into the form of an army, his future movements were determined for him by the Confederate proceedings, hereafter to be noticed.

The unlucky Pope was dismissed abruptly from Washington, and sent to an obscure command in the North-west against the Indians. M'Dowall, who had supported his chief, as he had M'Clellan before, to the very best of his ability, and had borne the chief share in the fighting at Bull's Run, now, for the second time, found his conduct unable to save him from the obloquy attending defeat. He was accused of imbecility, treachery, and cowardice, by the public voice; and that with such persistency, that he found it necessary to publicly resign his command, and demand a full inquiry, which he did, in words breathing the spirit of an honest soldier and high-minded gentleman. He was succeeded by General Hooker. Another corps, chiefly of Banks' troops, was made up for Reno, an officer of the old regular army, who had been distinguished for his activity throughout Pope's retreat. Of M'Clellan's former lieutenants, Keyes had retired from active service, and his corps was distributed among the others. Stoneman had also, for a time, left the army to recruit his shattered health; and the cavalry were placed under Pleasanton, a young officer reputed of much energy, but hardly matched against Stuart and his bold subalterns.

CHAPTER VI.

THE INVASION OF MARYLAND AND FALL OF HARPER'S FERRY.

CHECKED in the flush of pursuit by the works round Alexandria, the Confederate general did not this time renounce, as in 1861, the thought of improving the success just won. Lee and his Government thought that the time was come for abandoning the entirely defensive system hitherto employed, and making an advance across the line of the Potomac, open to them everywhere above Washington. If such advance should not be continued any great distance; if, as was feared, their resources did not permit the carrying a war of invasion into the better-peopled and deeply hostile North, two objects were yet before them. Maryland being entered by a Southern army after a succession of victories, would have the opportunity of rising to join that Southern cause, which her people were believed, in common with most of the inhabitants of the border states, to favour almost unanimously. A more direct military advantage might be obtained by the movement, and the consequent seizure of the railroad on the northern bank: for thus the numerous troops about Harper's Ferry and the lower Shenandoah, with the military stores they covered—which had been collected for new invasions in the valley—would be isolated entirely from Washington and Baltimore, and would fall an easy prey.

The drawback to the operation lay in the fact that the Confederates would, for a time, be dependent on a line of communication passing very near their enemies at Alexandria, and liable to be altogether interrupted. But they hoped to subsist their army for a time on the Maryland supplies, to be collected and purchased on the spot, not supposing that their doings there would meet with interruption from the army just driven back on Washington. They knew that the latter had been so demoralized by the late defeats as to abandon all their stores, and their wounded, to the number of 7,000; for these had fallen into the Confederate hands, besides the 6,000 prisoners and 30 guns, actually captured in the fighting; and they not unnaturally hoped that the shock lately sustained would prevent Pope's army facing them in the field for the present, and allow them time to carry out their designs abovementioned; and, if supported by the Marylanders, perhaps to operate against Baltimore, and interfere with the arrival of Northern levies at Washington.

With these views Lee lost no time in making the passage of the river. General D. Hill had brought him up the reserve, which, with the corps victorious at Bull's Run and some independent brigades, raised his actual force to 70,000 men. He directed his march by Drainsville on Leesburg, and crossed the Potomac, then low, at various fords near that place, on the 5th and 6th September. The railroad at Point of Rocks was instantly seized, its occupation isolating the Federal forces about Harper's Ferry completely; and the cavalry pressed on to Frederic, which place Lee himself reached soon after. The Confederates were received with friendliness, but without any special demonstration of joy, and when their commander proceeded to issue a proclamation calling on the population to rise and join the cause of the South, he met with no general response. The cautious border people, pressed upon by the weight of the great state of Pennsylvania—the frontier of which is but twenty miles from Frederic—and doubting much whether the Confederate invasion would prove more than a "raid," held back from public declaration of their views; and the recruits received into the Southern ranks were but a few hundreds. Lee did not, however, waste the time idly, whilst waiting to see the effect of his call, but proceeded to carry out his second object in a manner which proved completely successful. First pushing his cavalry on to Hagerstown, the terminus of a railroad which here crosses the Pennsylvanian border, and connects the west part of Maryland with Harrisburg, he directed them to advance on Chambersburg, twenty miles farther to the north, in order to induce the belief that he had resolved to carry the war in that direction. The device was successful; and the Governor of Pennsylvania, calling loudly for succour, ordered 50,000 of the State militia to take up arms against the invaders. M'Clellan at Washington, seeing the real danger, urged strongly the immediate withdrawal of the troops at Harper's Ferry: but his advice was neglected by the self-confident Cabinet, who, having recovered their first panic, were now engaged in raising the spirits of the North, by ridiculing the idea of their country being subjected to any real danger, from the ill-clad, half-famished soldiers of Lee; and underrated his power now as much as they had in the first alarm absurdly exaggerated it.

That general, in the meanwhile, despatched his active lieutenant, Jackson, on the 11th from Frederic with his corps, to effect the complete investment of Harper's Ferry. A single day's march brought them to Williamsport, where they crossed the Potomac, and directed their course next day by Martinsburg, on the threatened point. A considerable force of Federals had been stationed not many days before at the oft-disputed town of Winchester under Colonel White; but this officer, upon the news of the invasion of Maryland, had burnt the stores under his protection (destroying, from barbarity or recklessness, much private property), and retreated on Harper's Ferry, where his troops, joined to those of Colonel Miles, who there commanded, formed a force of 12,000 men. But these made no preparation for any attack, by taking up a concentrated position (as M'Clellan presently wrote them to do) upon one side of the river, nor attempted to force their way down the stream to meet the army advancing to their relief, so that they were instantly invested by Jackson on the south, and on the Maryland side by part of Longstreet's corps, detached for that purpose by Lee, under M'Laws. These arriving direct from Frederic, at the same time as Jackson appeared in the opposite direction, the operation was completely successful, save that some cavalry got away. Preparations were at once actively made for attacking the weak and extended positions the Federal commanders occupied.

We return to M'Clellan, who, on the 2nd, found himself in the chief command of above 90,000 men; for Burnside's corps, recalled from their useless expedition in North Carolina, were now disembarking in the Upper Potomac. No time was lost in redistributing the confused and mingled brigades, and the army was now organized in six corps, commanded by Sumner, Porter, Burnside, Franklin, Hooker, and Reno. Heintzelman remained in command at Alexandria, with his own troops and Sigel's. On the 7th, M'Clellan found his staff ready for field operations, his troops once more in heart, and a powerful train of artillery—albeit not as fine a one as that which he had carried to the peninsula—prepared to accompany him. His influence over the soldiery, his activity and organizing power, which can scarcely be too much praised, had for the time saved the Government he served from utter paralysis.

Two courses were open to him on moving out of the works into the field. An advance by the south bank of the Potomac would at once place all the communications of the enemy in his power. Hemmed in between his army and the hostile levies of Pennsylvania, Lee would be unable to subsist, and would infallibly have to recross the Potomac. He would have, moreover, to effect that operation in his enemy's teeth, with the risk of great disaster if he failed, and the certainty of much trouble in opening his way southward in any event but that of decisive victory. This movement, examined here by the light of subsequent events, appears to have promised results far greater than the other which M'Clellan determined on, and which was a direct march against Lee's army by the north bank. But the latter, as avoiding the passage of the Blue Mountains, appeared to lead more directly to the relief of the troops at Harper's Ferry, and would certainly be more acceptable to the frightened politicians of the North, who would have felt no security for their homesteads while the hostile army was between them and their own defenders. On it, therefore, M'Clellan determined, and so began his movement on Frederic at once.

When it is considered that there is but one main road to that town from Washington, and that one not such as would be considered of the first order in Europe, it will be apparent that the march of the army, with its large train, must have been at best exceedingly slow; and the reproach of tardiness made against the general falls to the ground, when it is found that the huge mass advanced at the rate of ten or twelve miles a day, until the enemy was neared. On the 11th, the Federal cavalry had some skirmishing with the Confederate outposts along the Monocacy, which was soon crossed, notwithstanding the destruction of the main bridge; and this was the prelude to the occupation of Frederic by Burnside next day, Lee having left it just before. The latter did not propose to retreat from Maryland and give up the territory north of the Potomac without a struggle, but it was necessary for him to delay the fighting a general action as long as possible, so as to give time for the divisions which surrounded Harper's Ferry to complete their work there and rejoin him. He moved, therefore, eastward, with some of Longstreet's troops who had been detached for purposes of supply, to Hagerstown; and passed through Boonesborough towards the South Mountain, where he had stationed General D. Hill and his 10,000 men as a rearguard, to check the Federal pursuit as long as possible. This general's command formed at this time a part of Longstreet's corps, which now included all the divisions, save the three belonging to that of Jackson.

It is evident that this movement of Lee's (who could not risk occupying a defensive position in front of Harper's Ferry till the passage was in his hands) by no means of itself gave shelter to Jackson from the advancing Federals, but rather uncovered the siege now conducted by him, by leaving the direct route to the invested post from Frederic by Jefferson open to M'Clellan. But the latter was understood to be greatly misinformed as to the strength of the Confederates, and his well-known character for carefulness made it almost certain that he would not press the flank move thus offered to him, at least while the passes in his front were occupied by them; but would proceed to clear these openings. This was rightly judged; and M'Clellan, following Lee direct with his whole forces, missed the occasion of relieving Miles and White. It would appear he might easily have observed the South Mountain with his leading corps, and marched the others on the Ferry; but he preferred a direct attack on what he took for the Confederate main army, to risking his communications in the least degree.

Though not very bold in their features, the hills in his front afforded a strong position. But Hill had not only to dispose his troops to defend the direct road to Boonesborough, but also to stop another pass where a second road, leading by the hamlet of Burkittsville direct to the passage over Antietam Creek at Sharpsburg, goes through the heights by an opening about seven miles to the southward. His force was so unequal to the task assigned, that he could not expect to do more than delay somewhat the advance of the Federals; and he had full need of the firmness which had been shown by him so remarkably in the first action of the war at Big Bethel, where he won his general's rank by a repulse inflicted on a greatly superior force, detached by General Butler from Fort Monroe.

On the 14th, at mid-day, the Northern army approached the hills from their last halting-place at Middleton. Reno's corps led the way, and was supported by Hooker's; for the firmness of the Confederates, and the strength of their batteries, imposed upon M'Clellan; and he believed, as has been stated, Lee and the greater part of his army to be in front. Reno attacked at about three o'clock with much vigour, and Hooker moved to his right, and gradually advancing up the hills, turned the position, and compelled Hill's retreat. The latter lost some hundreds of prisoners to Hooker's troops, but rallied his men on some of Hood's division who arrived from Boonesborough just before dark. The Federals, on their side, had to lament the death of General Reno, who had not long before pointed out to his staff the confusion caused in the Confederate ranks by the fall of one of their generals;—Garland, in fact, who commanded an opposing brigade, and who, strange to say, not many years earlier, was a friend and classfellow of Reno's at Westpoint.

The numbers under Hill, in this affair of South Mountain (or Boonesborough, as the Southerners call it), were vastly over-rated by the other side. But the error was in part due to the fact of his soldiers speaking of their general's "corps;" an error repeated by the journals, North and South, in their vaguely written reports. General Hill has not at any time commanded a *corps d'armée*, but his early services had somewhat singled him out, and caused his division to be specially maintained in great strength. This fact, and the character of the man—an excellent commander, but somewhat impatient of control—led to his being employed on this and some other lesser occasions in a manner almost independent of his immediate chief.

Whilst he now retired on Boonesborough and joined Longstreet, Franklin had carried the pass (called Crampton's Gap) to the south, on which he had been detached with his corps by M'Clellan; after a skirmish which lasted some hours, without much of real loss on either side. But M'Clellan's other corps were so much in rear of the passes, that, although he reported his success of the 14th as a complete victory, no effort was made next day to press on and cross the Antietam Creek only a few miles distant; so as to divide Longstreet from Jackson; or to interrupt the movement which the Confederate troops made along that stream to take up a defensive position, selected by Lee on its western bank, near, and in front of, the little town of Sharpsburg. Here he had a good passage over the Potomac, directly in his rear at Shepherdstown, and was in free communication with the forces at Harper's Ferry by the south bank of the river. The Federal leader made, indeed, a general advance, but too slowly to interfere with his enemy's operation. Some unimportant cavalry skirmishing took place about Boonesborough. The headquarters were moved to Keedysville, a hamlet on the west side of South Mountain, and to the south of Boonesborough. Hooker's corps proceeded to the latter place, followed by Banks' and Sumner's; Porter's and Reno's (now commanded by Mansfield) went more directly on Sharpsburg, by a cross road leading straight on Keedysville from the Gap (Turner's) where the chief fighting had been on the 14th; Franklin was ordered due south on Harper's Ferry from the point where he had forced his passage; but before he had made much progress towards the beleaguered garrison, a Confederate aide-de-camp was taken on his way to Lee, whom he supposed at Boonesborough, and M'Clellan learnt, to his chagrin, that the place he wished to relieve had that morning surrendered to the Southern general.

To return to Jackson, on the 12th, when he had completed the investment. The Federal troops, as we have noted, were strong in numbers, and they were fully supplied with the *matériel* necessary for a stout and protracted defence. But from the first they resisted without heart, and were commanded without judgment or tenacity. Colonels Miles and White, who seem to have divided the charge, attempted the occupation of the hills on both sides of the Potomac, taking up a position far too extended for their means in artillery and men. And they were opposed to a general who knew the value of every hour at this crisis of the war, and whose eye was too keen not to detect the errors and weaknesses of the defenders. Jackson, therefore, from the first, pressed them hard.

On the 13th, after a sharp cannonade, he directed M'Laws to lead his division against the more advanced of the Federal posts on the Maryland side; and a determined charge drove the Northerners, under Miles, from them so rapidly that they had

8

barely time to spike their guns before abandoning them, and retiring on a range of hills close to the river. Next day, the assault was again renewed—this time chiefly on the Virginia side—and with similar success; and before evening closed, Jackson had planted his batteries in each direction with such command as to reach every part of the now contracted position on the Northern side. On the 15th he reopened a heavy fire of shells, which had begun at dusk on the night before, to force a speedy submission; and the Federals at nine o'clock hoisted the white flag, and soon after entered into a capitulation on terms only short of surrender at discretion. Before, however, their signal was seen by the Confederates through the smoke of the batteries, Miles was struck and mortally wounded. In accordance with the usual custom of the Northern press, the defence of the Maryland heights was for a time declared to have been of the most heroic order; but the feeling of the army condemned the hasty surrender. The dismissal, by a military court, of two of the commanding officers of battalions employed under Miles, and the recorded charge, on the authority of this court, that the behaviour of the whole of one of the regiments was "disgraceful," show the stern truth too plainly for any present

THE INVASION OF MARYLAND. 115

doubt. General White, however, was acquitted of the personal charges laid against him.

The place having thus fallen, Jackson found himself in possession of immense stores, including 20,000 small arms and a great quantity of ammunition. His prisoners numbered over 11,000; and he took 60 guns. But he was too well informed as to M'Clellan's movements, and the result of the previous day's engagement at South Mountain, to be able to use his advantages fully. A struggle for the possession of Maryland was evidently very near, and although rumour, in giving M'Clellan 140,000 men, had no doubt enlarged, as usual, on the facts, yet Lee was certainly outnumbered, and would require every man in his army to meet the coming shock. Hurriedly, therefore, were the arrangements of the victors made. The prisoners were at once disarmed and discharged upon parole, according to the terms offered. This was, in any case, necessary, for guards could not be spared. The lighter stores, horses, and mules were sent southward up the Shenandoah, with a number of runaway slaves, who had been captured in the Federal lines. The other contents of the magazines were destroyed as speedily as might be, with the bridge of the Ohio Railroad lately repaired by the Federals; and these things done, Jackson moved his divisions, as fast as they could be spared, along the south bank, and so by Shepherdstown, on Sharpsburg. He reached the latter place after midnight on the night of the 16th, and immediately took up the position assigned him on the Confederate left.

CHAPTER VII.

BATTLE OF ANTIETAM.—LEE RETREATS INTO VIRGINIA.

WE return to M'Clellan, whom we left on the 15th at Keedysville, within five miles of the outposts of the Confederate position on the other side of the Antietam. He has heard the mortifying news from Harper's Ferry, and feels he has come too late for one great object of his march. But the same blow which thus broke his hopes of saving the great depôt and its garrison, set free, it was clear, the investing force that Lee had detached; and surely all the known circumstances pointed clearly to the necessity of an attack before they could reach the scene. Examining the proceedings of the 16th September, by the accounts most favourable to the Federal leader, there can be no doubt that the extreme caution which he then displayed (acting certainly upon very false impressions of the strength of the Confederates) caused him to throw away the opportunity of crushing the enemy, which the resistance of Harper's Ferry, brief though it was, placed fairly before him.

The river which divided the armies flows rapidly, and was too deep in most places to be forded. The ground on each side was of a rolling hilly nature; and on the right bank rises abruptly into a series of bluffs between the little town of Sharpsburg and the river. Along these bluffs Lee had posted his troops, carefully concealing their weakness (for they consisted of but a part of Longstreet's corps) by withdrawing them from the exposed parts of the heights. His numbers were fewer than any of his enemies supposed at the time; for the rapid marching of the advance from the Rappahannock to the Pennysylvania frontier, more than his losses in the battles with Pope, had reduced his army to scarcely 70,000 men; and the detached force now about to return from Harper's Ferry included 25,000 of these. Doubtless, therefore, he looked upon the delays of M'Clellan, who had his six corps, averaging 15,000 each, with a strong artillery and a few cavalry, making a total of certainly not much less than 95,000 men, within attacking distance on Tuesday early, as a most happy incident in his favour.

His position was approached by three bridges.

One in the centre laid straight from Keedysville to Sharpsburg; whilst lower down by nearly two miles another crossed the river, carrying a byroad which ran more directly southward to the Potomac. The approaches to both of these were commanded by the bluffs before mentioned. But the third bridge was nearly three miles from his centre up the stream, which there made a sweep away from the high ground and the line of the Confederate defence, thus giving an easy means of passage to their enemies.

Idly the latter seemed to allow hour after hour of the 16th to pass away. M'Clellan, unaware of the extreme disproportion of numbers existing all that day, took no more active measure for the whole morning than ordering some desultory fire from his advanced batteries, intended to force the foe to show their real strength. Meanwhile, he revolved his plan of battle, and decided that it should be as follows:— His right might cross over at the passage last spoken of first; and thus cutting the enemy off from the direction of Hagerstown, make a separate flank attack on their left; which, if successful, should clear some scattered woods to the north of Sharpsburg, and threaten Lee's retreat on Shepherdstown through that place. Hooker was to lead here, supported by Sumner, Franklin, and Mansfield. The latter (it should be said) was second on the general staff of the United States Army, when the Adjutant-General, Cooper, left the bureau, at the commencement of the rupture, to carry his talents and experience into similar office under the Southern colours. He had been employed in the head-quarter duties of organizing the levies, and had not served under M'Clellan in the previous campaign; but now having been appointed to one of the divisions lately organized, succeeded by virtue of seniority to Reno's command. The centre of his battle M'Clellan did not intend to press, the enemy's position in that part of his front appearing very strong, and the ground by which the bridge would be approached extremely open. He kept his cavalry here, and Porter's corps as a reserve; and a strong force of artillery played to occupy the enemy's attention, and prevent them seeing fully how the right had been strengthened at the expense of the rest of the line. Finally, Burnside, posted opposite the lowest of the bridges on the left, was to make a decided attack on the flank of the enemy in that direction, when Hooker had sufficiently advanced to threaten the other extremity of their position, and draw their strength that way.

By midday M'Clellan had made his dispositions; and seeing that the enemy refused to show their strength, and contented themselves with sheltering their troops from his cannonade in the hollows and woods on the rear slopes of the bluffs before mentioned, he moved Hooker's corps to the stream, with orders to cross at the unguarded portion by the upper bridge, and to establish themselves on the Confederate left.

Lee had now before him the problem so often presented to generals in the field for swift consideration and decision, viz. how to act in presence of an enemy evidently deliberately preparing to outflank him. No one of equal practical knowledge in war has discussed this matter so clearly and ably as the Archduke Charles, whose work, the ripe fruit of genius, aided by thought and experience, was doubtless familiar enough to the Confederate leader in those former days of quiet theoretical study, when he could little foresee what need he might find for such lessons. But, as has been shown, the numbers as yet in his hand were not the half of M'Clellan's, and he did not feel himself strong enough to deal with the emergency by striking a vigorous counterblow on the centre of the enemy's line, after Napoleon's example at Austerlitz; or by forming a new front on the threatened flank, unknown to the enemy, and ready to overwhelm the head of their advance, like

Wellington at Salamanca. All he could do, therefore, was slightly to strengthen his left, and busily occupy the woods and other cover on that side with skirmishers, hoping to detain the Federal advance long enough to give time for the arrival of the troops from Harper's Ferry.

At four P.M., Hooker had safely crossed the stream by fords above the higher bridge and quite beyond the Confederate range, and was slowly, but steadily, working his way upon their flank. Skirmishing soon began, and was continued hotly in the abounding cover until nightfall compelled its closing. The pickets of Hooker's divisions and Longstreet's slept so close to each other that the reliefs of the sentries actually met in collision more than once. Jackson arrived before daylight with a part of his force, his men pressing in so hastily to the ground as to be almost mistaken by their own friends for a new attacking force: he himself at once took command, as previously ordered, of the Confederate left; and Hood, with his division, who had hitherto maintained the defence of that flank, now moved away to guard the centre.

The morning of the 17th dawned bright, clear, and fraught with fierce interest. Armies of such strength as had never before encountered in open

BATTLE OF ANTIETAM.

field in the New World stood to their arms, preparing for the struggle which must decide whether the invading South should be driven back within her borders; or should see her army inflicting the trial of invasion on the hitherto tranquil interior of the North, perhaps retaliating for the excesses of Alabama, or the dull cruelties of New Orleans.

Hooker led off the battle, bringing his men into action with a personal bravery, which belied the notion that his well-known self-assumption and bluster were the mere outward show of a braggart. His reputation for courage dated, indeed, from the Mexican War; but his reported intemperate habits had kept him from early employment in this war, and only his strong personal solicitation of the President had procured him command in the army of the Potomac when first organized by M'Clellan. He had been known since for his readiness for action, and the good behaviour under fire of his division; but showed an impatience of authority, which separated him from his commander and militated against his usefulness. However, his *sobriquet* of "Fighting Joe" stood him in good service when once gained from the soldiers; and as we have seen, he succeeded M'Dowall in his command at the end of Pope's campaign; and that without objection on M'Clellan's part, who here selected him for the most important post in the opening of the battle. He had deployed his divisions during the movements of the afternoon of the 16th, and now entered frankly into the fight at their head. Jackson met him at once, and their troops encountered in a woody piece of country interspersed with small corn-fields, as soon as daylight broke; and fought for some few hours with very little advantage to either side. M'Laws' division joining Jackson early in the day, at the end of a forced march from Harper's Ferry, pressed back Hooker's left under Ricketts, and the Confederates gained ground for a time; but yielded it again as Sumner's and Mansfield's corps arrived to the support of the Federal attack. Mansfield, however, was mortally struck almost immediately after his appearance on the field, and Hooker, who exposed himself conspicuously to the fire of the enemy's rifles, was soon after wounded by a bullet through the foot, and carried off. With strange boastfulness (which later events show to be ingrained in the man's character), he marred the effect of his gallantry by a bombastic despatch addressed by him to M'Clellan, in which he claimed for himself the whole glory of the action, and declared that, if properly supported, he would have driven the enemy's army into the Potomac! Being dated from an unknown hamlet near the field called Centreville, this curious letter produced for a time the idea that he had fought a distinct battle from that in which M'Clellan's main army was engaged!

Hooker and Mansfield being thus removed, Sumner, with the gallantry that he had always shown, continued to fight with Jackson. His own corps now took for a time the leading share in the action, but, like Hooker's earlier in the day, it suffered very terribly from the enemy's fire. About noon, Jackson being further reinforced, directed a general charge, which broke Sedgewick's, the leading Federal, division, completely, and compelled Sumner to abandon the open patches of field about a small farmhouse where the chief struggle had been, and to withdraw his troops under cover, in order to restore discipline.

It was now past one o'clock, and the Federals held only the same woods which had covered them the night before. But their corps had not been all engaged. Franklin had now crossed the river with his, and arrived on Sumner's left, leading them as soon as formed against Jackson's men. The latter, exhausted and short of ammunition, were unable to meet this fresh shock: they gave way before the fresh divisions of Franklin; and these recovered the open ground so long contested, and even drove the

Confederate left half a mile beyond it: but not being followed by the remains of the other corps, did not feel themselves strong to press the advance towards Sharpsburg any farther; and the battle ended soon after two o'clock on this side, or degenerated into a harmless cannonade.

General Lee had but little work in the Confederate centre, where he held personal command; for the attack there expected did not take place, M'Clellan's plan not comprehending it, as we know. Porter employed his guns in constantly playing on the Confederate line, but this being well sheltered suffered but little.

Much later in the day than Hooker made his attack, M'Clellan directed General Burnside, with his corps of 16,000 men, to move against the Confederate right. It will be remembered that there was here a bridge over the river, and a road leading to the Potomac near Shepherdstown. Burnside's success would, therefore, seriously threaten the line of retreat which Lee desired to cover. Doubtless, M'Clellan hoped that the perseverance of his attack on the right might have caused his enemy to strip this part of his line, and thus lay himself open to a decisive blow. But Lee was fully aware of the importance of this passage, and had charged Longstreet to guard it in person with a part of his corps, in strength nearly equal to Burnside's. The attack was extremely slow, the Confederates availing themselves of every small piece of cover to defend the approaches to the bridge; so that it was two o'clock before Burnside had crossed it, and begun to move up the hilly ground beyond. For a short time only his divisions continued their advance; when General A. Hill arrived to reinforce Longstreet with the last troops from Harper's Ferry, and these two, uniting their forces, moved steadily forwards against Burnside, and drove him at once over the half mile of ground which he had gained back to the bridge; so that he was from this time reduced to the defensive. About this time of the day it was that M'Clellan, having sent an order to his right directing Franklin's attack to be more vigorously pressed, received from Sumner the positive assurance that it could not be executed without great risk to the corps, inasmuch as none of the others in that wing were in any condition to support the advance. The two Federal attacks were, therefore, now completely paralyzed. Yet M'Clellan had close to him Porter and his 15,000 men, who had been all day under shelter, and were quite fresh. These, however, he did not dare to employ on either flank, so much did he fear a counter-attack upon his own centre by some hidden reserve of the enemy. The later afternoon wore away, therefore, amid some sharp skirmishing about the bridge which Burnside held, and some desultory fire from batteries in other parts of the field. The battle closed with these; for M'Clellan until dark expected some such movement of his enemy as that just referred to; and Lee knew well that his wings had exhausted all their strength, while his line in the centre had never been more than sufficient to hold the naturally strong ground where it was posted. The demand for Jackson's support had at the beginning stripped it of all the troops that could possibly be spared. The ammunition, too, on his side, had fallen short, as happened so often to his army.*

Next day the armies remained facing each other in the same positions as they held in the midday previous, and, like two exhausted gladiators, respected each other's repose. In fact, the Federal general has since distinctly stated that, with the

* "In all these battles," writes an officer who served in the Confederate Staff in Virginia and Maryland, and who has afforded much valuable information for this work, "our ammunition gave out; we had no horse-feed; and our men also were short of food. These were the causes of our inability to take advantage of victory." But a friend of the author's recently received from one of the chief Southern generals the confession, that this inability was also greatly the result of the want of discipline in the army—a want partly, but not by any means entirely, supplied by patriotic feeling.

exception of Porter's, no corps in his army was in any state to be led to a fresh attack. On the other hand, the Confederate army was reduced by the losses in the late engagements to a strength of less than 60,000 men; and it was evident to Lee that with such inferiority of numbers, and far as he was from reinforcements, to assume an offensive part would be beyond his means. Nay, as he knew well that M'Clellan would soon recruit his army from the large levies now hurriedly being made in Pennsylvania and the adjacent States, his own safest plan was clearly not to expose himself to the risk of being attacked again by overwhelming numbers, with the Potomac in his rear, but to effect his passage of that river whilst the enemy were not yet recovered from the exhaustion of the late struggle.

He made his preparations at once, sending off his stores and baggage all day and in the night; and on the 19th early commenced to break up from his position, and cross the Potomac into Shepherdstown. A convention had been entered into the day before for the burial of the dead. Three hundred of the most seriously wounded were abandoned to the Federals. With the exception of these, the operation was accomplished without any loss.

M'Clellan's army had by no means recovered from

the sort of stupor in which the battle had left them; and he was compelled to abandon the hopes he had doubtless entertained—hopes which the untrustworthy telegrams of Washington and the scribes of the Northern press had exaggerated into certainty—of some striking success to be obtained over the enemy in their retreat. The invasion of Maryland was over. Pennsylvania was saved from the lately threatened inroad. Washington politicians might breathe once more freely. But in these short statements were comprised all the advantages the Northern side gained in the recent struggles.

The Battle of Antietam is essentially one of the most indecisive of great contests; and each side, naturally enough, laid claim to a victory. As the result of the fight was the final abandonment of their position by the Confederates; as the right wing of the Federals had never lost the ground gained by Franklin's advance; and as some of the Confederate standards and nearly a dozen guns had been captured in this and the previous attacks by Sumner and Hooker on that side of the field; M'Clellan had good grounds for asserting that he had met with great success. And to have accomplished as much as he had done; to have restored enough of confidence to the beaten and demoralized mass he led from Washington to enable them to face, not unsuccessfully, the lately victorious enemy; to force the triumphant Southerners to their own side of the border, and abandon their grasp of Maryland;—these achievements must ever reflect credit on M'Clellan. But inasmuch as the Confederate general had retained his position for nearly forty-eight hours after the battle; had retired unmolested and without hurry, taking everything with him from the ground, but one damaged gun and a few hopelessly-wounded men; above all, as the great military object of the invasion, the capture of Harper's Ferry, had been successfully accomplished, General Lee may well also lay claim to have gained a solid advantage.

The Federal losses in the battles of South Mountain and Antietam (or Sharpsburg, as it is called in the South) amounted to about 2,300 and 12,500 respectively, as we are informed by General M'Clellan's report. But it is not an easy task to fix accurately those of the Confederates. In the report just mentioned they are estimated at 30,000; but the suppositions on which this number is calculated will not bear examination. One of them is clearly that all the muskets picked up upon the ground were Confederate property; yet the number of killed and wounded on the Federal side would cover nearly the whole 14,000 which were brought in. Nor is there any reason to believe that the Confederates lost at the two battles any great number of prisoners beyond the 1,200 wounded left in the hands of the Federals, and who were included under another head in the list of casualties. Again, as there can be no more leisurely retreat conceived than that of Lee, who occupied five days in the few miles between Middletown and Shepherdstown, so M'Clellan's assumption of nearly 5,000 stragglers left by his enemy in Maryland appears entirely fallacious. It is true that one of his staff reported 3,000 Confederate dead to be buried on the field of Antietam, and probably the general accepted this statement as correct; but as his forces in the attack, made partly over open ground, lost only 2,010 killed, and as all accounts agree that the Confederate artillery on this occasion was numerous and well served, it is matter of positive certainty that the defenders must have lost considerably fewer; and the number returned must be taken as largely exaggerated by the superintending officer. It is well known that nearly all the Confederate wounded were safely taken into Shepherdstown within twenty-four hours after the battle, and of these only 1,000 remained in the vicinity of that place a fortnight afterwards, as has been stated by an impartial witness, a volunteer surgeon from the North, who visited the hospitals there on the 3rd October with a pass. From these circumstances, with the analogy to other defensive battles fought on difficult ground, and the positive assertions of all Confederate authorities, we may deduce the fact that the total Confederate loss (exclusive of Jackson's at the Ferry) was considerably less than that of their assailant, and certainly under 12,000 men.*

The loss in general and field officers in these battles was very considerable on both sides, and argues that the troops required much encouragement and leading. Besides Mansfield and Reno killed, the Northerners had twelve other generals on the list of wounded. Their enemies counted six or seven disabled, and had to regret the deaths of Generals Garland, Branch, and Starke—the last at this time serving in the division formerly Jackson's, and still bearing the title of "Stonewall," won under their old leader at Bull's Run.

* A gentleman on the medical staff of the Confederates at Antietam assures the writer that the return of 2,000 killed and 6,800 wounded covered the whole loss. Allowing for a few hundred prisoners, and adding a loss at South Mountain (or Boonesborough) equal to M'Clellan's, we arrive at a total of 12,000 nearly.

It has already been pointed out that M'Clellan's numbers would have authorized his moving direct from Frederic on the 13th towards Harper's Ferry, detaching a sufficient force to hold Lee meanwhile in check; and that his ignorance of the latter's numbers is plainly the only excuse for his not having done so. His delay on the 15th and 16th, is also a blot upon his conduct of the campaign. Nor can the tactics employed by him in the momentous battle itself escape censure. The exhaustion of his troops—in great part recruits—on the right wing, in the middle of the day, was a certain consequence of the early hour at which they were engaged. The Prussian staff in the wars of 1813 and 1814 were so well aware (says Müffling) of such a general fact, that they always avoided engaging their young levies until late in the day; and M'Clellan's own experience, independent of any theoretical rule, should have taught him the same. The consequence of this being overlooked was, that when Burnside began to press the Confederate right severely, the battle of the Federals was, as we have seen, confined to his attack; and this, to have had any hope of success, should have been made before that on the right had so completely broken down.

But there is another serious charge against

M'Clellan beside that of making his attacks so disconnectedly that they afforded no help to each other. We have seen that he kept 15,000 men in strict reserve to the very end of the battle—a force which, properly employed, might have been used to obtain some decisive advantage. For any practical effect produced on the 17th, or the next day, Porter's corps might as well have been at Washington. There is no example of any great tactician thus making useless his superiority of force of his own choice, except the single one of Napoleon refusing to employ his guard to decide the desperate struggle at Borodino; and although the great Emperor had the strongest possible reason for thus reserving his best troops, in the enormous distance from his depôts which he had arrived at, and the consequent impossibility of replacing them; yet he has been more condemned than admired for this striking deviation from his usual practice, which rendered his victory so indecisive, and ultimately so useless. But M'Clellan was in the very reverse of such a position, and could have had no similar reason; for his reinforcements were near, and those of his opponent exhausted. The only excuse which can be made for his timidity as to the use of his reserve, must lie in the ignorance he laboured under as to the great numerical inferiority of Lee. But, at the best, there seems something wanting here; and we must judge the event to have shown that his caution at Antietam, as in former instances, was so excessive as to rob him of any chance of brilliant success.

Those who are disposed to be over-critical, may accuse Lee of having needlessly fought the battle of the 17th. Indeed, it would seem that he was so little pressed on the two preceding days that he might, as soon as the news of the success at Harper's Ferry reached him, have retired over the Potomac without being harassed to any serious extent, and have joined Jackson at Shepherdstown. He cannot, therefore, be said to have fought in order to complete, in security, the merely military objects of his expedition. But to have abandoned Maryland on the mere appearance of M'Clellan, would have injured materially the prestige of the Southern arms; and he might well believe his strong position would prove impregnable against the attacks of those soldiers he had lately chased so rudely through Virginia. Moreover, any decided repulse of the Federal attack, ending in a retreat vigorously followed up, would have left him master of the north side of the Potomac for months, and able perhaps to distress the Northern Cabinet most seriously by the occupation of

Baltimore. He played, therefore, for a great stake; and but for the power which M'Clellan wielded over the Federal soldiers, it seems probable that he would have won.

CHAPTER VIII.

THE FOURTH INVASION OF VIRGINIA.—M'CLELLAN SUPERSEDED.

As Lee slowly withdrew his rearguard on the 19th September, under cover of batteries planted round Shepherdstown to sweep the north bank of the Potomac, some of M'Clellan's lighter artillery followed up the retreat and exchanged a few idle shots with the distant guns of the enemy; but the day passed away quietly on the whole. The Confederates had accomplished their movement most successfully; and the dreams of their demoralization and probable destruction, which the Washington telegraph had so busily circulated in the substantial form of official reports, gradually passed away with the harmless smoke of the firing.

No one who knows M'Clellan personally seems to doubt that, at this period of the campaign, the despatches circulated under his name, which appeared to express his belief in the speedy destruction of Lee's army, were invented, or at least were greatly altered, from the originals. Indeed, the previous telegrams, communicated by the War Department as from him, were totally contradicted by two published on the 19th September. In the first of these the General states the plain truth that he did not yet know whether the enemy were crossing the river; while in the second, only written some hours later in the day, he at last claims "a complete victory" for the Northern arms.

Next day he seems to have imagined, from the quiet on the southern bank, that the retreat of his enemies would be continued without delay up the Shenandoah valley; and he directed a part of Burnside's and Porter's corps to attempt the passage of the river at a ford near Boteler's Mill below the town, which appeared to be but weakly guarded. Barnes' brigade accordingly crossed, supported by one of General Sykes' regulars; and seeing the gunners flying in apparent confusion from some light field-pieces which had been shelling their advance, they rushed boldly forward to capture them, unmindful of the disaster which, under like circumstances, had befallen Baker's force at Ball's Bluff just a year before. Yet the same dangerous enemy was watching them. Jackson, to whom Lee had intrusted the guarding of the river, had his whole corps carefully concealed behind patches of wood and rising grounds in the vicinity of the fords. A heavy fire of artillery was suddenly brought to bear on the advancing Federals, and checked them instantly. General A. Hill's division followed with an attack directed in flank as well as front, which drove the troops that had crossed back upon their supports and towards the ford in panic and disorder. The three leading regiments, New Pennsylvanian troops, were killed or taken almost to a man; the rearmost only recrossed under cover of a heavy fire from the batteries previously planted to protect their passage to the attack. The repulse, in short, was so bloody and decisive that M'Clellan ceased for a while the attempt to pass into Virginia, and collected his army at various points of passage, where he held them still, awaiting the reinforcements which daily came in.

Meanwhile, his adversary, aware of the increasing strength of the Federal forces, withdrew the bulk of his troops to a defensive position not many miles from the Potomac, behind a little river called the Opequan, which runs northward and empties itself into the former between Williamsport and Shepherdstown. His right, commanded by Longstreet, was thus thrown back towards Winchester, whilst the left reached nearly to the Potomac, and was under Jackson, who, with Longstreet, had now been raised to the rank of lieutenant-general, and divided with him the charge of the whole infantry of the army, thus consolidated into two large corps. The cavalry formed a separate division under Stuart, and were chiefly employed in patrolling the country in front of the army towards the passages of the river.

M'Clellan had thus the option of crossing at Harper's Ferry or Shepherdstown, and establishing himself firmly at the entrance of the valley. But his usual caution seemed rather increased by late events, and it was evident that no advance into the interior could take place without either exposing a flank to Lee's army, or at once attacking him in his chosen position, and that with the Potomac in the rear. This risk M'Clellan was determined not yet to run, although most urgently pressed by the Washington Government to make some decided movement. They had now just issued their proclamation, proclaiming the emancipation of all the slaves in the hostile portions of the South, and were anxious to give it some practical effect by assuming the offensive. The inaction of their principal army, after its late partial success, seemed also to contradict the assumption of victory which they had so loudly made, and might influence the forthcoming State elections unfavourably to the Republican party, whose support was given them on the implied condition of maintaining the most earnest prosecution of the war. The instructions of their organ, Halleck, for M'Clellan's advance, became therefore the more urgent; but the latter had learnt experience as to the danger of having his operations controlled from a distance, and positively refused to cross the river until his demands for reinforcements, and completer stores for the forthcoming campaign, were fully complied with. He remained, therefore, motionless, awaiting the men and supplies he had called for.

During the latter part of September, the country to the south-east of Alexandria had been entirely denuded, by the call of Lee for more troops to add to his main force, of the Confederate detachments left there during the Maryland campaign. This compelled the Confederate army to confine their line of supply entirely to the valley, and deprived them for a time of the direct use of any railroad. All the stores, &c. required were brought to the head of the Shenandoah by the Virginia Central Railroad, and carted from Staurton down to Winchester, a distance of ninety miles, by a service somewhat resembling those employed for transport in Europe, but carried on, as will be imagined, under great difficulties. So light, however, were the demands of Lee's troops, who had drawn much provision from Maryland during their short occupation, and gained greatly by the supplies found at Harper's Ferry, that the system was employed successfully for some weeks; the weather, it should be remarked, continuing unusually fine, and giving great facilities for cartage.

Meanwhile Sigel's troops, left at first with Heintzelman's at Alexandria, had been gradually and cautiously pushed out through the scenes of Pope's late disasters, and their advance reached the Rappahannock without opposition. The want of enterprise, so remarkable in the Federal leaders, was here strikingly illustrated; for, although their weakness might have been a sufficient reason for the forces at Alexandria not attempting any movement along the south of the Potomac during Lee's invasion of Maryland; it certainly does appear to reflect discredit upon them, that during the several weeks that he remained upon the Opequan, not a single attempt was made to interfere with his long line of supply by an incursion into the valley through any one of the numerous passes of the Blue Ridge. In several places, it is quite certain, his commissariat must have conducted their convoys within a few miles of Sigel's outposts: nor does it appear clear that M'Clellan had not the power at least of ordering an attack to be made in this direction. Had the Federal side possessed such an officer as Jackson, stationed with even a small force so near the enemy's communications, we cannot doubt he would have made Lee's position, at the mouth of the valley, quite untenable.

A full month wore by after the affair of Boteler's Mill in complete inaction, save as regards the cavalry of the respective armies. On the 2nd October, General Pleasanton crossed the river near Shepherdstown, with several squadrons and six light guns, to make a reconnaissance in force. He soon fell in with a brigade of Stuart's cavalry under F. Lee,[*] who retired, skirmishing, before him towards Martinsburg, and were slowly followed up, until they reached a position behind the Opequan. News of the enemy's approach to the Confederate lines had been duly despatched to Stuart himself, who soon appeared, and moved up another brigade (Hampton's) to the support of that under Lee. Pleasanton, seeing him-

---

[*] There are two brigadiers under Stuart of the same name—viz. General Fitzhugh Lee, nephew, and General W. Lee, son of the Commander-in-Chief of the Confederate army.

self outmatched, at once gave the word to retire, and fell back on Shepherdstown : he was closely pursued, but brought his squadrons off without any great loss, covering them well with his guns, and manœuvring them through the retreat with a degree of order highly creditable, considering his inferiority in numbers, and the quality of the opponent he had to escape from. His rearguard was driven in by a smart charge just before he reached Shepherdstown; but it was then nearly dark, and, though dispersed, most of them escaped the enemy's hands.

On the 10th of the month the Confederates proceeded to return the visit of Pleasanton. But Stuart, not content with merely reconnoitring, planned and carried out a cavalry foraging expedition, such as the annals of war can scarcely match for boldness and success. Leaving the army of Lee by its extreme left, he moved secretly up the river Potomac, and crossed, about ten miles above Williamsport, into Maryland at its narrowest part, with a battery of light artillery, and about 1,500 of the best mounted horsemen in his three brigades. Passing through a village called Mercersburg, a day's march brought the adventurous band to Chambersburg, an old Pennsylvanian country town, about twenty miles north of Hagerstown on the railroad from Harrisburg to that place. The local authorities were duly summoned, and assured of good treatment for themselves and their properties; and the latter were perfectly respected, according to the Southern policy in Maryland during the late occupation: the horses only, which Stuart much needed a fresh supply of, were treated as implements of war, and seized by his troopers; whilst all forage and provisions taken were paid for in paper. These facts are substantiated by the narratives of the Pennsylvanian residents. They are the more noteworthy, because one of Stuart's brigadiers at Chambersburg was the same W. Lee, whose family seat at White House (inherited by him through General R. Lee's marriage into the Washington family) had been destroyed in the Federal retreat from the Pamunkey in the previous June. His loss was well known among the troopers he commanded. But most of these were men of superior birth and education; many of them of good Virginian families, and under the control of high feeling. Lee himself, being reminded by one of them of a hasty vow of vengeance made at the time of the occurrence, declared that he would never follow the bad example the Northern troops had set of carrying on a war like barbarians.

Nor did the Confederates stand in need of any

private booty; for in the town were found large Government stores of clothing and ammunition, as Stuart had been informed; the capture of these being, indeed, one chief object of his expedition. At daylight he busied his force in preparing to move, taking with them as much of the more useful part of the spoil as their horses, ridden and led, could carry. But the alarm had been spread by the telegraph, notwithstanding the rapidity of his advance, and he could hardly hope to return by the direct route which had brought him to Chambersburg. He despatched, therefore, General Hampton's brigade at early dawn on Gettysburg, a town about twenty-five miles to the eastward, at the source of the Monocacy, with orders to seize such Federal property as he might find, and to use all possible precautions to prevent the movement in that direction being reported. Later in the day, he followed with the rest of his party, having carefully destroyed all the stores they could not remove, and released on parole the wounded, who, to the number of 300, were taken in the hospital. The first part of the night of the 11th was passed by Stuart's head-quarters at Gettysburg; but, after a few hours' rest, he pressed his command rapidly down the Monocacy towards the Potomac, passing by the left of M'Clellan's army, and traversing a road which leads nearly due south to the Potomac. A march of forty miles brought him to that river at a place called Edwards' Ferry, not far from Leesburg. As he approached the stream, General Pleasanton's cavalry appeared in view, having marched up the Potomac to watch the upper fords upon the first news of the incursion, and now down the stream upon exacter intelligence. But their horses, always ill-kept and overworked, were too much exhausted by their long march, and the force actually in hand too few, for any interference with Stuart's passage. The discharge of a single ill-aimed gun by the Federals served but to mark the completion of the gallant exploit, and the Confederate leader re-entered Virginia, bringing 600 fresh horses, and clothing sufficient for his whole division, the latter being a boon specially acceptable to his somewhat ragged soldiery. In the complete circuit he had thus made round the rear of M'Clellan's army, he had marched a distance of ninety-six miles without the loss of a man; he had surpassed his own former feats on the Chickahominy and Rappahannock; obtained a most seasonable supply for the wants of his command; and inflicted considerable damage, and more than proportionate annoyance, on his baffled foes.

Meanwhile, M'Clellan's force had been much

increased by additions of regiments from the 300,000 volunteers (for nine months' service only) lately called for by the President. His requisitions for supplies had also been fully met ; and he prepared for a new campaign. The army under his immediate orders now numbered over 140,000 men, intended to be divided into nine corps, (of which seven actually existed,) besides Sigel's, hitherto detached ; and, about the 20th October, a new organization of it was ordered (instigated, no doubt, by the restless jealousy of the War Department), preparatory to the intended movement he announced. The whole were to be distributed into three grand divisions, of three corps each, commanded respectively by Sumner, Burnside, and Hooker—for the latter had recovered from his wound. This arrangement, which appears at first sight to be a return to the system in vogue before Napoleon, of dividing large armies into the three separate commands, right-wing, centre, and left, appears to have been nominally adopted rather with a view to lessen the incessant references made by the corps' commanders to the general-in-chief, than with the assumption that, as a field system, it was any improvement on that hitherto used, which was taken (as before remarked) from the model of the armies of the First Empire. The three chiefs of the grand divisions were, therefore, authorized to correspond directly with the War Department—a permission certainly calculated to save their immediate superior much trouble, but, at the same time, so sure to injure his needful authority, that it would hardly long be borne by any general of spirit.

M'Clellan, however, was not easy to offend, nor to turn by petty affront from his purpose; for he now saw the time arrived for acting with safety against the enemy with an army which he knew would follow no other leader with confidence. He had completed all his arrangements, and had gradually moved the bulk of his troops below Harper's Ferry, which might now be considered as the headquarters of his right wing. He had resolved not to plunge the mass of men he commanded into the Shenandoah country. He judged that if Lee should be attacked, and should retire up the valley after an indecisive action, the Federals in pursuit would find the supply of their unwieldy army by that narrow line almost impossible, after they once left the railroad at Winchester; for their wants would be far larger than their enemy's, and the country presented still to them the difficulties incident to the invasion of a hostile territory. Abandoning this notion of forcing Lee back by directly crossing into his front, as the Washington

Cabinet would have desired, he resolved to dislodge the Confederates by moving to his own left, skirting the foot of the Blue Ridge, and following it down towards Manasses Gap, whence he could use the Orange Railroad for his supply. His large force, which was independent of the troops specially intended to protect Alexandria, afforded the means of closing the passes into the Shenandoah on his right flank effectually, and yet of making a formidable advance in the Richmond direction; and by moving deliberately, and forming depôts as he went, it was hoped the one railroad might be made to serve his needs. It was certain that Lee would not allow him to proceed any distance between himself and Richmond, and that, therefore, his advance would have the first desired effect—viz. the causing the Confederates to break up from the Opequan position, where their presence seemed a constant menace to Maryland and Pennsylvania.

All things being in readiness, he commenced his movement on the 23rd October. Burnside, with the right, crossed on pontoon bridges at Harper's Ferry, and leaving a strong division there under General Geary to watch the passage, followed the centre and left grand divisions (*armies* they were at this time denominated), which passed the Potomac chiefly about Berlin, a village fifteen miles lower down, in their march southwards. Strong detachments were thrown out on the slopes of the Blue Ridge to cover the operation, which was undisturbed; and was yet not completed until the 29th, for it took six days to carry over the stream the immense mass of encumbrances which followed the different corps. Slowly the invading host wound its way round the base of the hills above Leesburg, and thence southward along their slopes towards Thoroughfare Gap.

A series of skirmishes of the slightest nature drove the Confederate outposts successively from the several intervening passes known as Vestal's, Snicker's, and Ashby's Gaps. At the end of the first week in November, the Manasses Gap Railroad was occupied up to its entrance into the valley, with scarce any resistance from the enemy's detachments near Front Royal; Warrenton was entered by the advance of the main column; and M'Clellan had the satisfaction of ascertaining that his first object had been attained. Lee's army, in fact, as had been calculated, broke up from their advanced position so soon as they knew certainly the purpose of the Federal advance, and retired up the Shenandoah, their general moving rapidly on Staunton and Orange with the bulk of his forces, to interpose between M'Clellan and the country south of the Rappahannock. Having made this parallel movement, and passed his slower enemy, Lee occupied his old position of the previous August between the Rapidan and Rappahannock. The troops with him consisted of Longstreet's corps, formed of five strong divisions, commanded respectively by Anderson, Ransom, M'Laws, Pickett, and Hood, and forming the bulk of the army; and the cavalry. Jackson and his three divisions (under the two Hills and Early) remained in the valley south of Front Royal, and threatened M'Clellan's right flank. The whole position of affairs, therefore, was not unlike that existing when the movements to outflank Pope by the mountain roads were begun in August; but M'Clellan's strength, and the precautions he had taken, preserved him from any like attempt. Whether he could have continued his advance as successfully beyond the point he had reached—whether he had forces and skill sufficient to press Lee's army back from his front towards the oft-threatened capital it covered, and at the same time continue to guard effectually the line he moved and subsisted by, as it lengthened—whether, in short, he could ever have reached Richmond by the path he had now at last chosen,—these are questions left to calculation or conjecture. The Washington Government had determined to remove him from the command of the army of the Potomac, and on the 7th November the order arrived for him to transfer it to General Burnside; which being at once done, he retired for awhile into private life, bidding adieu to his troops in an address so modest in its tone, and withal so well-chosen and stirring, as to extort admiration even from his political enemies of the press.

For long there had been, as has been shown, a mutual distrust between himself and the authorities of Washington, growing partly out of their original ill-support of him in the peninsular expedition, and partly from a general and avowed difference of sentiment as to the manner of conducting the war. M'Clellan had never concealed his abhorrence of the bloody and desperate counsels of the extreme Abolitionist party, into whose hands the President was gradually more and more falling. To this feeling was now added a deep-seated jealousy of his influence with the soldiery on the one side, and a most natural contempt for the imbecility of the Administration on the other, a contempt which many of his supporters among the military avowed too loudly. That he had taken command almost without instructions of the beaten troops of Pope, and had rolled back the tide of invasion from Northern soil, were circumstances that aggravated the breach. He had been compelled, indeed, as matter of military duty, to put down the habits of political discussion which had increased in his army to a great extent after the Antietam success; and had done so most loyally, be it said, although the feelings he thus repressed the expression of, fully harmonized with his own, and were directed against that part of the Cabinet which was avowedly hostile to him.

The difficulty thus existing had been brought to a climax by the November elections in the North. The ballot-boxes in the chief States had told so unmistakably that the feeling of the country was with the General and against the President, that a rupture was almost unavoidable. Many journals called loudly on M'Clellan to seize dictatorial power with armed hand, and overthrow the despised and unstable Government; others threatened the latter with the withdrawal of the whole Republican party's support, unless they dealt at once severely with the General who was betraying his country's interest by his lukewarmness. Thus attacked by both parties, the President was urged by his most trusted advisers to take the decisive step (as indeed he had been some weeks before by the delegates from a meeting of his chief supporters among the State governors); and the whole

Cabinet, Seward excepted, having added their weight to the pressure, the order for the supersession was signed on the 6th November, and at once despatched to Rectortown, near Manasses Gap, the then headquarters of the General, who, acting with his usual prudence, lost no time in leaving his excited army. The nominal cause assigned for his dismissal was his delay to cross the Potomac the first three weeks subsequent to the battle of Antietam; but the mere dates proved this not to be the real charge, and the correspondence published on that subject for the justification of the Government only showed his praiseworthy firmness, in refusing to risk the army without receiving what were, in his view, necessary supplies. His chief friend, Porter, was relieved at the same time from the command of his corps, and ordered to Washington to stand a trial for his alleged misconduct under Pope;* not that the Administration cared so much about crushing him, as that they hoped to make use of the proceedings, conducted as much as possible by their creatures, to throw discredit

---

* He has since been dismissed the service, as before remarked. But Pope's own evidence on the trial seems to confirm Porter's statement, that the non-appearance of part of his corps in the first day of the great battle at Manasses was due to the mistakes of the brigadiers, and not to any will of his, who himself appeared with the rest. There is reason to fear that the verdict of the Court was predetermined.

indirectly on M'Clellan. In the same spirit, the committee appointed by the Republican majority of the Congress to inquire into the conduct of the war, strove for months after his removal, by every means unscrupulous animosity could suggest, to leave upon the general the blame of past ill-success. But their efforts have been in vain. A tendency to over-caution, carried, at times, to its extreme, remains proved as a charge against him, as these pages have already sufficiently illustrated. But, on the whole, his conduct shows in most favourable contrast to the presumption, rashness, and cruelty chargeable against so many other Northern leaders: his private character for honour and probity appears above all suspicion; and there still remains to him the exclusive credit of the only great campaign which the Federal arms can claim as a success—the re-conquest of Maryland.

CHAPTER IX.

BURNSIDE'S CHANGE OF BASE.

As the telegraph wires flashed through the land the words of the simple, manly address in which M'Clellan took leave of his army, they told also that his successor assumed his new charge "with diffidence;" and men naturally inquired on what grounds he had been chosen for so weighty a post. A few months earlier, Burnside had only been known as one of the most fortunate of the many retired military men, whom the commission of a State Governor had suddenly elevated from obscurity into the rank of a general officer. His six years of former employ as subaltern in the regular army, would bear no comparison with the long and active service which Sumner and Hooker had seen previous to this war; even should no regard be paid to the severe trials they had passed through with honour in the late campaigns. Nor were his political principles more acceptable to the Cabinet than theirs, he being, at that time nominally a Democrat. But he had the advantage of his name being unconnected with the disasters which had befallen the armies of the Potomac and Virginia. His easy conquests of Roanoke and Newbern—small posts on the coast of North Carolina—had been magnified, by contrast with other men's defeats, into great achievements. He was young in years; reported active, bold, and careful of the comfort of his troops; and when the President named him to his high office, it was thought by the Ministry that he would be more easily controlled than either of the two veterans whom he seemed to supersede. On such grounds, therefore, the selection was made, and hailed with acclamation by the Government organs as the forerunner of success.

He at once carried out the new organization of the army which had been enjoined upon M'Clellan. Franklin was named to succeed him in charge of one of the "grand divisions." Porter's removal and this promotion being promulgated, the seven corps originally put in motion were distributed into six, and two of each of these formed one of the principal commands. Sigel's corps, which had been acting separately, had some other troops allotted to it, and his authority, as commander of the "grand reserve," was made equal to that exercised by the chiefs of grand divisions, in independence of the general commanding—an independence certain, unless most judiciously employed, to interfere with the proper working of the army as a whole. This arrangement, indeed, was only one step removed from the original vicious Federal system of sending separate armies to operate in the same portion of the hostile country. Sigel's duty was specially to watch over the flank and rear of the army on its intended advance, and preserve its communications: and this his former experience of that part of Virginia was thought to qualify him for, though his want of enterprise made him but a poor opponent to the swift attacks to be expected from Jackson and Stuart.

To carry out these matters of detail was simple enough. Now came the question, how should the army be moved? Should Burnside attempt the operation which M'Clellan had apparently kept in view, of advancing steadily on, trusting to his superior numbers to force Lee from the line of the Rappahannock, and then to follow him southward? or should he try some other mode of approaching his object? For this one had the special disadvantage that, after passing Gordonsville, the bend of the railroad to the east would compel any invader who followed it, to make a long flank march thence to Hanover; and to do this in the face of such an army as Lee's was now known to be, and one led by such a general, seemed to be courting defeat. M'Clellan, doubtless, had had his plans for overcoming this and the other difficulties of the way; but his reticence had prevented their being divulged. It was evident, however, that immediate action in some direction was a condition of the command in the present temper of Government and people; and Burnside at once made up his mind to abandon the attempt to proceed by Gordonsville, and to transfer his army to the railroad from Acquia Creek—at this time only thirty miles to his left—in order to try that route, hitherto quite unused, except by M'Dowall at the time of the peninsular campaign.

As the Rappahannock lay between him and the Confederate forces, there was no great difficulty nor danger in transporting his army by the flank movement from the one railroad to the other, and putting it upon an entirely new line of operations. The change would also involve some certain advantages; for Washington being still regarded as the base from which the movements on Richmond were to be made, the distance along the new railroad was scarce half of that by Gordonsville, and the bulk of the supplies as far as Acquia Creek would be carried by water with the most perfect facility, and without fear of interruption. The railroad was also not only shorter, but it ran perfectly direct by a southward course to Richmond, and thus the danger of flank movements in an open country was avoided. It was plainly also easier to guard from the dreaded surprises of Jackson, being not only so much less in length, but being well removed from the dangerous vicinity of the Blue Mountains. Moreover, his proximity to the Potomac would enable the new general, as he thought, to distract the attention of the Confederates from his real purpose by some feigned preparations (which were made indeed afterwards, but without effect) for shipping and transporting his army down that river to land them near Richmond.

To balance these considerations, the march down the Rappahannock to Fredericksburg (which is fifteen miles below the junction of the Rapidan with the main stream) would put a large deep part of the river between the armies, and it might prove no easy matter to force a passage in the face of the enemy. However, Burnside fondly hoped that his own state of ignorance as to the Confederate movements might be equalled by theirs as to his own, and that his leading corps might arrive before Fredericksburg, and cross into that town, before the Confederates could have a sufficient force there to check the operation.

Accordingly, the army began its march eastward on the 12th and 13th November. Sumner led the way, followed by Franklin and Hooker; whilst Sigel was charged with the occupation of the country which the Federal main body was quitting, and his command was to be disposed to cover their right flank and rear. The cross-roads to be used on the march were so few and bad, that the former general's corps did not reach Falmouth, a suburb of Fredericksburg on the north bank of the Rappahannock, until the 17th. He then summoned the town to surrender, as he had been directed by Burnside. But the Confederate troops of Longstreet had been marching by a parallel movement, having discovered at once what their enemy designed; and the town was already occupied by them in force, so that all hope of crossing by surprise was lost to the Federals. Fredericksburg itself is completely commanded by some woody heights which run along the northern bank of the stream, and might therefore be crushed by the fire of artillery to such an extent as to render its defence impossible in face of the powerful batteries arriving at Falmouth. But the real position of the defenders of the passage was plainly on another line of hills south of the town, and also within range of it: and the demand made by Burnside on the 21st for the surrender of the place, accompanied by a threat of bombardment in sixteen hours if not complied with, argued him greatly ignorant of the customs of civilized warfare, as well as of the real difficulty of the attempt he purposed; for the evacuation of the town by its unfortunate inhabitants led in no way to his advantage. The women and children were indeed removed —the time allowed being, at the request of the municipality, extended to forty-eight hours—but the Confederates still occupied the buildings with their advanced posts, and declined, of course, to assist him in approaching any nearer his object, by allowing him to pass his troops over unopposed, as he seems to have expected.

The bombardment, however, was deferred, and the armies remained facing each other for nearly a month without any movement of importance. The Confederate general had returned, it seemed, to his favourite system of keeping strictly on the defensive; unless some incautious movement of his adversary should lay him open to attack. Burnside, on the other hand, was detained in his present position for want of any effective means of transporting his troops

BURNSIDE'S CHANGE OF BASE. 165

over the very obstacle which his own march down the river had placed between the armies. Pontoon bridges were positively required to attempt the passage with, yet week after week passed away before he was provided with the needful equipment for throwing them over the stream.

So much has been said of this same deficiency of pontoons, that it is as well to refer to it in detail as a striking illustration of the manner in which the Northern war has been misconducted. Burnside, it appears plainly from the correspondence lately published, had written, on assuming his command, to General Halleck, to announce his intended movement to Fredericksburg; and demanded that the bridge train which had been employed near Harper's Ferry should be forwarded thither at once. So badly did Halleck conduct matters at head-quarters, that he took it for granted, without inquiry, that Burnside would send some officer of his own staff to superintend the required transport. Burnside did not do so until he discovered that no progress was made in the matter; and when the pontoons were at last despatched, they were sent overland by the very indifferent roads from Alexandria, causing a further delay of many days in their carriage. Amidst mutual recriminations between chief and lieutenant, one arrives clearly at the simple conclusion that each was incompetent to the onerous duties which lay on him. And it should be noted that these blunders were not made—as in that Crimean war so sharply criticized by American officers—at the commencement of hostilities, but at the end of eighteen months of war conducted on the very largest scale.

The Federal forces, though not in movement, were by no means suffered to remain during this interval in perfect quiescence. The cavalry of Stuart, now posted at all the fords along the Rappahannock, crossed frequently, in their usual bold style, into the enemy's lines. Pleasanton did his best to check their incursions, but found his raw troopers utterly untrustworthy when out of his own immediate view, and scarcely dared make the necessary detachments to watch the various cross-roads by which the enemy might be expected. Especially was his arm of the service brought into discredit by the capture of two whole squadrons of a Pennsylvanian regiment of cavalry on the 28th November. These cavaliers were employed at an out-station near a crossing on the Upper Rappahannock; but kept their watch so ill that they allowed Hampton to dash into their post with part of his brigade, and to surprise them before they could mount, and, on his summons, surrendered without striking a blow. The same Confederate leader, on the 11th, and again on the 16th December, crossed the line of road between Alexandria and Fredericksburg, at the village of Dumfries, a chief halting-place for Burnside's waggons, and made on each occasion a capture of a large convoy, with its guard.

General W. Lee was no less active below Fredericksburg, turning his troopers into boatmen for the time, and carrying on sudden assaults, by means of skiffs, on the enemy's pickets on the opposite bank. In one of these forays near Port Royal, twenty miles below the town, he carried off an entire picket of forty-nine men and officers, with their horses and arms, and brought them over to the Southern side without losing a man of his brigade.

But Burnside had other stimulants to action more powerful than these annoyances inflicted on his extended line. The Federal Government had pompously announced that they had reinforced his army by all the "veterans" available; and had, in fact, brought from their numerous coast expeditions several thousands of soldiers who had been enlisted early in the war, and might be supposed to be better drilled than the recruits who formed the bulk of the army of the Potomac. The latter now numbered not less than 125,000 men, exclusive of Sigel's reserve; and Burnside well knew that he was expected to do more with such a host than to spend the winter idly in face of the enemy. He had received no order directing him to force a passage in their teeth at any risk, and took the resolution to do so, he has since avowed, entirely upon his own responsibility. But he doubtless well knew that inaction would not be long endured by the seemingly complaisant Cabinet, and still less by the Northern press:—the latter, indeed, had already flagged somewhat in its adulation of his high qualities of command. He saw no other way of advancing on the line he had selected; and the pontoon train (the delay of which had hitherto excused him from moving) having arrived, he gave orders, on the 10th December, to pass the river at all available points near the town the following morning, under cover of the whole of his artillery.

The Confederate army had now been nearly a month united in his front; for Lee had ordered Jackson in from the Shenandoah on the first news of the movement upon Fredericksburg, and that general arrived safely with his whole corps by the 26th Nov. No detachments, except a few of the cavalry, were made; for Lee fully foresaw that the concentration of the Federals would prove the preparation for a battle, and judged he had need of his entire force. His infantry divisions, eight in number, had been strengthened, and averaged, including the artillery belonging to them, 10,000 each. Adding to these Stuart's division of cavalry, and allowing that of about 4,500 troopers (including horse artillery) under this general's command, one quarter at least were at too great a distance to be brought in on sudden notice, we find that nearly 85,000 men occupied the position of which it is intended to speak fully in the next chapter.

CHAPTER X.

FREDERICKSBURG.

It has been said that the town of Fredericksburg, which lies in a small plain, is completely dominated by some bold hills on the northern bank. These are called the Forest Great Heights; and along them the Federal batteries being posted, brought the town, and the low ground adjacent, under a heavy fire at their general's will. But on the southern side also run a range of heights, approaching at first within a quarter of a mile of the outskirts of the town, and afterwards receding from the stream with a gentle curve as it flows downwards to the east. The plain thus formed between hills and river is about two and a half miles across at the widest part, where the former are broken by an opening, through which the railroad to Richmond makes its way. To the east of this, the ground rises again into a long line of hills called the Highlands, which approach the river and closely follow its course far down, meeting it first at a point about five miles below the town. The hills in front of Fredericksburg were nearly bare of trees; but passing along them to the Confederate right, across a little brook called the Hazel, which breaks them about a mile from the town, their face is covered in places with thick oak copse. The trees had been left standing, and thus the Federals were unable to see the strength of the entrenchments with which Lee had covered the weaker parts of his line: at the same time, the cover thus left seemed to afford some facilities for the attack. Such was the position which Lee calmly occupied for some time previous to the actual assault of Burnside—a position so good, and manned by troops so devoted, that he hoped, rather than expected, that the Federal general would cross to attack it by main force.

On the 11th, however, as we have seen, the passage commenced. Three pontoon bridges were prepared at early dawn, under cover of a fog, at different points opposite the town. Franklin was directed to throw two more across the river two miles lower down; and he succeeded in doing so without much opposition before the day had far advanced, and prepared to cross with his, the left grand division. It was intended that Sumner with the right, followed by Hooker with the centre, should pass into the town early in the day; but the fog having cleared up at this part of the scene before the engineers had finished their bridges, some sharpshooters—at first two companies only, but afterwards strengthened by several detachments from their brigade—kept up so deadly a fire from the buildings opposite as to compel the work to be for a time abandoned. Burnside, who had watched the proceedings in person, about ten o'clock directed every gun which could be brought to bear upon the houses to open, and drive the riflemen from their cover; and for nearly an hour and a half the air was rent by the roar of thirty-five batteries, numbering 180 pieces — many of such calibre as no army in the field has ever used before this present war. The unhappy town was shattered, torn, and fired, until it seemed to the spectators to be changing into a huge column of dust and smoke. But the bombardment failed in the effect desired: the gallant riflemen—part of a Mississippi brigade under Barksdale—lay unmoved by the wounds or death which struck each moment some comrade around them: and when a second attempt was made about noon to form the bridges, they resumed the galling fire, and stopped it at once.

Colonel Hall—an old soldier who had seen the

first shot of the war fired at Fort Sumter—now offered to cross part of his brigade in some large boats which had been brought to the spot that day by land, and drive the enemy out. Receiving permission from Burnside, he called for volunteers, and obtaining 400 readily from a Michigan regiment, headed them boldly in the passage. The feat was daring in its way, even under the protection of the batteries, and deserved the success it obtained. The boats, ten in number, were rapidly pushed over, and, after a short struggle, the defenders of the buildings were driven from the water-side, fifty of them being captured.

The completion of the bridges was by this single act of bravery rendered easy, for Lee's batteries did not open fire. He was fully aware that he could not hinder the passage being accomplished; he had never been deceived by demonstrations made by parties of the Federals far down the river; and with the sagacity that marks his judgment, he scented his adversary's desperate purpose and certain defeat, and desired not to offer further impediment to his forming his army on the southern bank. He busied himself, therefore, only in securing victory for the coming struggle: but judging that Burnside would probably make his attack on the Confederate right—

where success alone seemed possible—he spent his pains chiefly on that side of the ground.

Here Jackson was posted with his corps; Earley's division—commanded by that general since Ewell had been disabled at Bull's Run—was on the flank of the infantry of the whole army, beyond the opening of the hills, where the railroad passes through them at a spot called Hamilton's Crossing.

The cavalry and their light guns covered the space on the extreme right towards the river. A. Hill's division was next to Earley's on the Confederate left of the railroad. D. Hill's division—counted still the finest in the army—was held in reserve to these two; for Lee anticipated a severe pressure upon them. For the same reason their front was also completely swept by heavy batteries hidden by the trees. On the Confederate left, and opposite the town, was placed one of Longstreet's divisions, under Anderson. Ransom, M'Laws, and Pickett were posted next in succession; and the line was filled up to the position of Jackson's corps by the division of Hood, who had won his major-general's rank by his gallantry in the temporary command of the left wing at Antietam. The extreme left of Longstreet, like Jackson's right, was especially flanked by carefully posted batteries. The slight separation made by the Hazel Brook of this part of the line from the left centre, seemed to render this the more necessary; but a strong stone wall ran along the lower part of the heights on this side, and formed a ready parapet for the defenders. In short, no part of the position was so open but that the Confederate officer in charge of it felt himself able to resist any attack which might be directed against him; while a force of artillery, which counted nearly 300 guns— for in this arm the Confederates were no longer inferior to their foes—was so admirably disposed as to render an approach to any part of the intrenchments impossible, save under exposure to a crushing fire.

The Federal staff not only remained in entire ignorance of these details, but were unaware even of the general extent of the preparations for their reception. Particularly they seem to have been misinformed as to the force of guns opposed to them, not knowing how diligently Lee had used the railroad from Richmond to bring up a mass of artillery of the heaviest calibre. Burnside himself had made up his mind to try the issue of a general attack on the whole line of the enemy, and to throw the special weight of the assault on the bare hills opposite the town, called Marye's Heights; for here the indentation caused by the Hazel gave him, as he hoped, the opportunity of severing the Confederate left. He had founded this resolve on the opinion —how conceived it is difficult to say—that he had so far deceived the Confederates by a feeble demonstration made lower down the river towards a place called Fort Conway, as to lead them to place the bulk of their troops in that direction, on the Highlands. He intended to employ his batteries opposite the town in firing over it to cover the main attack; and these he hoped would much aid his design, for the hills at that point were within fair range. To prevent aid being sent to the Confederate left, he would move a number of batteries, well supported by troops, upon the enemy's centre, at the wider part of the plain. A vigorous attack by Franklin, in a direction parallel to the river, on the extremity of the Highlands to the Federal left of the railroad, would be sufficient, he thought, to occupy the enemy's right effectually.

The plan of Burnside was fully discussed in the presence of his three lieutenants; as, indeed, the anomalous position they occupied scarcely allowed him to act without their concurrence. As usual in like cases, opinions and counsels varied greatly; and although none knew exactly what might be the numbers of the Confederates, or the strength of their works, yet there was a general misgiving as to the result of the experiment. Hooker expressed this feeling with characteristic vehemence: nor can it be doubted that had the rest of the generals known the full difficulties they had before them, and that the attack was really to take place against a strongly-entrenched camp, guarded by 80,000 men and mounted with the heaviest guns, their remonstrances would have been so loud as to have changed the purpose of their chief. But Burnside, strong in his belief of the enemy's dispersal along the river, argued that the assault being made with numbers so superior upon a line of such great extent, some single point would certainly be carried, and the rest of the defences thus made useless. With the true obstinacy of a narrow mind, he clung to his one idea, thus misapplying a rule good in itself. He forgot that to take a continuous line of works, it is necessary not only to enter somewhere, *but also to keep the point thus gained* within the *enceinte*.

Many are the instances in war where a part of the defensive position of an army, ranged on a long line, has been for the moment carried; but the success not being properly followed by support, or the defenders having brought up their reserves more quickly than the assailants, the latter have been cast out again, perhaps with heavy loss. Such was the fate of the advance of Junot's corps, at Busaco, after it had fairly penetrated the English position on the crest of the hill. No less unfortunate was the issue of the bold attack made by the centre of the allies upon Napoleon's works at Dresden, though it succeeded for a time. But as striking an instance of the uselessness of this kind of temporary advantage occurred more recently at the hill held by the Allies at Inkerman. There a Russian battalion, having crowned the heights unopposed, at an unguarded point, deployed, halted, and melted away again down the slope without any pressure, being timid and distrustful of their advantage from sheer want of support.*

To return to our narrative. The discussion just mentioned, which was taking place on the 12th December, did not interfere with the preparations for the passage of Burnside's whole force. The bridges had not been completed until 5 P.M. the night before, and no attempt was made to use them for more than crossing a sufficient body of Sumner's leading corps (the 2nd, under Couch) to occupy the town in strength, and cover them effectually. Two

* This circumstance is given upon the authority of a distinguished officer, then upon the staff, who witnessed the scene from an uncomfortably short distance, he being at the time entangled by his horse, which was shot under him not far from the Russians in question.

miles lower down Franklin had performed a similar operation with part of Reynolds' troops, though without buildings to protect his advance. But he was not molested seriously by the Confederate skirmishers; for the southern bank was there completely swept by his guns, and the point of passage (which was at the mouth of a small brook called Deep Run, intersecting the plain rather lower down than the Hazel) was beyond the range of the batteries opposed to him.

Next day an attempt was made to bring Sumner's columns down the face of the hills behind which they had encamped, to the bridges; but their leading sections were found to be so exposed to the shells from Marye's Heights, a few of which were directed at them, that they were withdrawn under cover for the present. Burnside prepared, however, to effect the passage before daylight next morning, and concentrated the mass of Franklin's and Sumner's commands as close as possible to their respective bridges. Much skirmishing of a very desultory nature took place this day on the southern side; and the Confederate outposts withdrew towards their lines, leaving Franklin to connect his pickets with those of Sumner. The Federals thus occupied a strip of the southern bank which lay between the town and Deep Run, and which the Hazel divided in the middle. Some distant and irregular shots aimed at the various masked points of the Confederate lines from the guns on Forest Heights, were occasionally replied to by the Southern artillery; but in such a guarded way as rather to conceal by their smoke the hills behind them, than to show where the strength of the works lay: they failed, therefore, of their object, and the day passed by without Burnside discovering how his adversary had occupied his ground.

The morning of the 13th December, which both armies awaited in the dread suspense which goes before great battles, proved so dark and foggy as particularly to favour Burnside's design of passing the main body of his army over unseen. The passage was pressed at all the bridges, and soon the little plain in their front was filled with masses of armed men, interspersed with guns. For four hours this operation went on undisturbed, save by the delay and confusion which, with troops so large a part of whom were raw, was unavoidable; for frequent was the mixture, in the obscurity, of battalions, and even brigades, with other bodies of different divisions. So great was this delay that when, just before nine, the mist began to lift, and to reveal the movement plainly to the enemy, the whole of Sumner's second corps (the 9th, under Wilcox) was not yet brought across.

The Federal soldiers behaved steadily, and moved in as orderly a fashion as could be expected, whilst the staff strove to rectify the confusion. But upon the spirit of officers and men lay the dead-weight of doubt as to the power of themselves or their general to accomplish the task so rashly entered on. It was whispered everywhere that Hooker — a man whom his worst enemy had never known to blench from danger—had denounced the movement as foolhardy. His tongue had, as usual, outrun the discretion of that general, and made known the divided counsels of the day before; and the rumour spread and carried fear from corps to corps.

Far different was the feeling of the Southern army. Something of anxiety, stretched for long hours of expectation, was in the breast of every man who, through the fog, listened impatiently for the expected sound of approaching attack. But new troops and old were confident in their position, their leaders, and themselves; and the anxiety was rather to know on what precise part of the line the shock might fall, than any fear of its effects.

It is not intended here to follow out in detail the bloody scenes of the tragedy that ensued. There is no lesson to be learnt in tracing out the minor features of a slaughter—rather than a battle—the whole course of which must reflect indelible discredit on its author. Following the main facts only, it is necessary first to say that, about nine o'clock, the skirmishers of Franklin's columns engaged those pushed out by Jackson into the plain. Here General Bayard, second in command of the Federal cavalry, was mortally wounded early in the fight, and fell much regretted; for he was an officer of great promise (though untrained before the war), and bade fair to raise the character of the arm he had to deal with, and of American volunteer generals. At ten, the plain was cleared of the fog, and the batteries of the Federals opened on the enemy's position with a heavy, but not hurtful, fire; whilst, about the same time, Sumner advanced Couch's troops against Marye's Heights, and the battle of musketry began round their base also. He also pushed Wilcox's corps, as soon as it had crossed, to his left; and they occupied the ground as far as the other side of the Hazel, joining Franklin's right. At noon a general advance was attempted; but the brigades which led only drew near the hills to meet so terrible a storm of grape from the batteries, and bullets from the deadly rifle-pits which lined the front of the works, that they not once could anywhere reach the line of intrenchment. In vain the officers called them on:

such a fire as this would have staggered Napoleon's old guard, or Picton's peninsular veterans—for even brave and tried soldiers are but mortal—and they came on only to turn again and again, and strew the ground with their dead and dying. Meagher led his brave Celts—the remnant of the Irish brigade, which had fought so well at Gaines' Hill, and shared the hot struggle with Jackson at Antietam—nearly to the muzzles of the guns on Marye's Heights, but only to fall in such heaps as to give the confined spot they charged through the gloomy name of the "Slaughter Pen." In the centre, Ferrero, with one of Wilcox's brigades, gained the hill for a moment; and near this part, the Confederates gave ground, and a battalion of A. Hill's men — new conscripts from North Carolina—turned and left their line; but a reserve brigade, of Early's division, was instantly moved up, and the Federals repulsed and chased, as after each of their unsuccessful attacks, far into the plain beyond. Lee had arranged the defence of his works so that they were manned by not much more than a third of his force; and the other troops were kept under cover, but sufficiently ready to fill up instantly any gap that might be made, or to follow up the retreating foe. Occasionally, the bolder companies of the Federal columns would enter and cling to some of the patches of wood at the lower part of the hills: then some of the Confederates from the rear of the works were launched at them, and drove them forth into the plain again, where they must needs fly hastily from the crushing fire of the guns. On the whole, the Northern regiments behaved well; but it is not surprising that before the afternoon wore by, their attacks had almost ceased: although Hooker's two corps (the 3rd and 5th, under Smith and Slocum) had now passed through the town, and deployed to support Sumner's exhausted troops. At five, the battle had died away into an irregular cannonade; and in this the Confederate gunners, well posted behind rough but efficient parapets, and, for once, abundantly supplied with ammunition, had naturally an extreme advantage. Indeed, for some hours previous, it had been impossible for Franklin to press his attack; for soon after noon, having pushed his left division—commanded by Meade, of Reynolds' (the 1st) corps—against the hills near Hamilton's Crossing, he witnessed the entire rout which befel them in arriving at a point where, entering the curve of the heights, they were met by a concentrated fire on their front and flank. Jackson, the general of the leading brigade, was killed in the attempt to rally them: and the panic produced by

FREDERICKSBURG. 185

their flight being added to by the constant attacks which Stuart, with his horse artillery, directed along the river against the flank of the corps; the whole of the latter, as well as Stoneman's (the 6th), which was acting in support, was paralyzed for any offensive movement.

The battle was closed by a last attempt made by Wilcox on Marye's Heights, which he now essayed to carry by turning it. He directed Hawkins, with his brigade of Getty's division, to ascend the Hazel, under cover of the dusk, in hopes that he might succeed in taking in rear the defenders of the hill. But the men were in no heart for such a night attack, nor could they proceed far enough without discovery to turn the end of the wall, which had checked Couch in the several attacks made early in the day, on the front of the hill. On receiving a fire from some of the division of M'Laws, who occupied the east slope of the height, the Federals halted, returned a few straggling shots, and retreated in disorder.

Twelve thousand killed and wounded of the beaten army lying on that small plain, and 800 prisoners taken by the enemy, attest the greatness of the sacrifice made in Burnside's experiment. He gained by it simply—as he states in his despatch three days after the fight—the knowledge "that the position in front could not be carried." Doubtless his soldiers regretted that he had thought fit to purchase this so dearly at their expense; and the fact that he himself directed the movements all day from the opposite side of the river, did not serve to make his conduct more palatable in their judgment. Certain it is that their irritation and despondency after the defeat were so intense, that any attempt to renew the assault would have led to a wholesale mutiny—if the reports of their officers are to be believed.

The Confederates lost on their part, at the most liberal estimate, barely one-fifth the number just mentioned. This great disproportion takes the battle at once out of the category of such great defensive actions as Waterloo, Borodino, or any other with which the reader might be at first inclined to class it, stamping it as a special example of hopeless, murderous waste of life; and marks the general who forced it on, with the brand of a most fatal rashness. Nor was his work less faulty in the details of its execution than in the general design. Burnside neglected the facilities afforded by the wider portion of the plain near Deep Run for forming his huge host for a decided general attack on the Confederate centre or right; and leaving Franklin there unsupported, made his chief efforts from the open ground in front of the town, which was not only fearfully swept by the flanking batteries of Longstreet's left, but so narrow that the corps of Sumner had no room to form. Their commander, though an excellent leader of a division, and brave to a fault, had not sufficient head to rectify the error of his chief; and thus they were thrown away in driblets by separate assaults made by single brigades in the most unconnected and random fashion, and perished or fled without any influence on the position they attacked. How completely the right bore the brunt of the Federal battle, we learn from their losses in killed. Many corpses were removed privately the two nights following, it is positively asserted by the Confederates; but of those actually counted three days after, two-thirds had fallen in Sumner's attacks. The other third belonged chiefly to Franklin's two corps, for those of Hooker, as has been seen, were not much exposed to fire.

Turning to the Southern general, it seems sufficient to point to the complete result obtained by the success of his dispositions, and at so small a cost. In fact, no fault has been found by friend or foe with the way in which Lee concentrated, sheltered, and fought his army on the 13th December. But some praise should be spared to his admirable lieutenants. Jackson—whose element seemed to be in the storm of battle that raged along his front, and who, in personal valour, judicious care of his troops, and entire devotedness to the stern business in hand, seemed (as he had before shown at Manasses and Antietam) to be no less great in defence than attack. Stuart—the very model of a cavalry general entrusted with the flank of an army: whose light artillery performed such admirable service under their young chief Pelham, the boy-hero,* since prematurely cut off: and whose only difficulty was to restrain his own ardour and the eagerness of his division, lest they should be tempted into broken ground within range of the enemy's heavy guns, and the army suffer in its trusted scouts. Longstreet perhaps most of all—whose corps this day showed the same unshakable front and confidence in their chief, which had marked his men ever since he first commanded a brigade: and whose own conduct, ever conspicuously shining in battle, testified how well Johnson had judged of him long before, when he had marked him out on the Chickahominy as "a general almost

---

* Pelham was killed about three months later in an obscure skirmish near Culpepper, at the age of twenty-two, having risen some time before into command of the horse artillery of the whole army.

infallible in an emergency:" and Lee, when he had said, in answer to the President's question as to his fitness for a certain duty, "Longstreet is competent to fill *any* position in the army."* With such supporters as these, no wonder the Confederate chief appeared—as all report declares—the very embodiment of calm dignity and confidence, while he watched the development of the Federal attack.

Whilst the victorious host passed the night in some expectation of receiving a fresh attack next day, many hours were not needed to tell Burnside the feeling of his troops. Indeed, he was informed by Sumner, in the plainest terms, on proceeding to order that general to make a renewal of his attack next morning, that any continuance of the assault would, in the opinion of every general officer in that wing, lead to certain disaster. Franklin, being called from his post, strongly confirmed this view; and conviction at last flashed on the general-in-chief's own mind, and made it clear that instant retreat was advisable.

A proposal of Burnside's to withdraw a part of the army only, leaving the freshest of the corps to hold

---

* The writer has these anecdotes of General Longstreet from a gentleman high in the present official employ of the Confederate States, who has lately conversed on the subject with President Davis.

the bridge-heads and the position of the 12th, was so loudly opposed by Hooker (whose two corps would have been those isolated by this arrangement), that it was at once abandoned as no less dangerous than remaining altogether. Indeed, the three subaltern generals appear at this period of the campaign to have practically taken the guidance of affairs out of their commander's hands. It was resolved, therefore, to make a general transfer of the whole force to the northern bank as soon as might be.

But to execute such a movement was not so easy as to determine it should be done: for the bridges near the town led, as we know, to a slope exposed to the batteries of Marye's Height, and so could not be used in the daytime. Nor would it do to attempt to concentrate on Deep Creek; for the passages which had with difficulty served for Franklin, would be insufficient for the whole army. It was plainly, therefore, necessary—when Burnside had once made up his mind to receive as truth the facts of his position—to conceal the intention of retiring as long as possible, and to occupy the ground on which the wretched soldiers had passed the night after their defeat, with as firm a front as might be. They would then take advantage of the first opportunity presented for escape, if it were found that the enemy did not venture from his works, and bring on an engagement in the open ground.

This Lee had no mind to do : and, on the contrary, he occupied his men in further strengthening their position; for he was unaware of the hopelessly depressed condition of the Federal soldiery, and with all his principal generals, Stuart excepted, thought it probable that they would again risk an assault. A few cannon-shot only disturbed the quiet of the day; which was calm and warm, and was succeeded by a night so still, that Burnside did not attempt the retrograde movement, which, he felt, would be detected inevitably, and might lead his adversary at once to attack him. Meanwhile, the dead lay unburied, and the unhappy wounded of the Federals filled the air with their groans, as they lay perishing near the works they had assailed : for Lee had been tricked by an unauthorized request of one of M'Clellan's generals into granting permission to enter the Confederate position, after the battle of Antietam, and remove the dead and wounded under a flag of truce ; a concession which the Northern reports (since their commander had not himself asked it) had made appear the consequence of the loss of the battle by their opponents. He resolved, therefore, to communicate with no one but Burnside himself;

and refused a flag sent in by one of his subordinates, Birney, who commanded a division of Hooker's.

The 15th passed by nearly as quietly as the day before. Those generals of Lee's army who had thought at first that the silence boded a fresh attack preparing, now began to doubt if this rest of their enemies were not really a sign of exhaustion amounting to impotence. But he still determined not to give up the advantage of his impregnable position, and even went on with the works begun the day before. He also relaxed somewhat of his first severity of intention; and moved by the intense sufferings of the enemy's wounded, suffered their removal from beneath his guns, without waiting for the formal request in Burnside's own hand which he had demanded, and which did not arrive till the 16th.

Before evening the wind had risen, and at dark increased to a gale, bringing heavy rain. As it blew from the south it quite prevented the Confederate pickets from hearing any but the very loudest sounds from the camp of their foes; and Burnside lost no time in commencing the passage of the river. In this he exerted himself greatly; and although the night was long, his bridges — now completed to six in number — excellent of their sort; and the movement greatly concealed by the other favouring incidents referred to; it still reflects a certain credit on him, that before daylight he had transported the whole army, with their guns and baggage, to the opposite side without the knowledge of the enemy.

But in the escape of Burnside's forces from their critical position lies a blot on the judgment of the Confederate general, such as justice forbids us to pass by. It may be urged that the imperfect state of discipline inherent in the Southern armies would of necessity prevent their pickets, on so stormy a night, from duly observing what their enemy was about. In this way we may excuse the fact of the complete escape of the Northerners by their nocturnal flight; or, at least, palliate the seeming carelessness which permitted it.

But the question still remains unanswered,—Why did Lee allow the two days succeeding the battle to pass by without making a counter-attack upon his enemies, still staggering from their repulse? It is true that the lives of his men were far more precious to their country than those of Burnside's to the North. It is true that he could only conjecture—what we now well know—the utterly dispirited condition of the Federals. But something must ever be risked in war, where a very great object is to be attained; and in this case of Fredericksburg, as in most others, the old rule appears to hold good, "That the basis of sound defensive action is a readiness to take the offensive at the right opportunity." Had Lee, on the morning of the 14th, thrown his whole force frankly against the Northern army, reduced as the latter was in numbers, and much more in *morale* by its severe repulse, it is scarcely to be doubted that a mighty advantage would have been obtained. The mere beginning of any panic among Burnside's troops would have inevitably caused them to sever their line, by yielding to the natural tendency to fall back on the different sets of bridges that had carried them across; so that, an advantage once gained, the weight of the Confederates might have been directed almost wholly upon Franklin, or upon the other two grand divisions. It is possible, indeed, that the scenes of Leipsic or the Beresina might have been repeated on the Rappahannock, and the greater part of the Federal corps have been captured or destroyed. It is possible also that the political results of such a defeat might have reached scarcely less far than those which followed the disasters of Napoleon just quoted. Finally, when we assert thus plainly that Lee at Fredericksburg erred from over-caution, and missed an opportunity of further advantage, such as even a great victory has rarely offered, it must be borne in mind that his troops were not on this occasion suffering from over-marching, or want of food and ammunition, as in former cases, which the reader will recall. To attack or remain still was, therefore, strictly a matter of choice; and judging after the event, with that fuller knowledge which time brings, we are enabled confidently to say that the decision should have been more bold.

Of the remainder of this campaign there is, indeed, but little to be said. A special committee was appointed by the Senate to inquire into the particulars of the disaster; the object being to allay the popular disgust and indignation. Burnside for a time preserved the favour of the Ministry by fully taking upon himself the responsibility of the fatal passage. But his authority in his own army had already passed away from him beyond recall. Hooker led the opposition against his commander; and such a state of dissension arose, that the latter, on the 23rd of January, issued a remarkable general order, openly censuring Hooker and eight other of his generals. The immediate cause of the dispute was an attempt made by Burnside on the 20th January to surprise a passage above Fredericksburg by a flank movement to his right; which bad weather, and perhaps the ill-will of his subalterns (for Hooker violently remonstrated against the attempt), turned into one miserable scene of failure and confusion. It became necessary for the President to interfere in the matter, and he made his decision by removing Burnside from the command in which he had so notoriously failed, and appointing as his successor his insubordinate lieutenant. For, indeed, he had but little choice in conferring the vacant post; as Hooker seemed to be the only man, save M'Clellan, in whom the army appeared to put any trust.

Franklin was relieved from his command with Burnside; for under the latter's control he had been often charged with tardiness and failure in carrying out his orders. He retired, therefore, from service, pending the inquiry which he demanded. Sumner also, disgusted and suffering in health,[*] resigned his charge and left the army. The latter, therefore, came under the guidance of an entirely new staff, and the system which had divided it into three several commands was soon after abandoned; so that Hooker obtained direct control over his chiefs of corps.

He found it, however, easier to take his new

[*] He died a few weeks afterwards, at the age of 72.

powers than to use them. Facing the victorious army of Lee, he discovered as yet no way of solving the hitherto unsettled problem of the advance to Richmond; and the rains of early spring coming to his aid, with their accustomed swelling of the rivers, and destruction of the roads, he accepted, doubtless thankfully, the delay. So, with the exception of some cavalry "raids" of Stuart's, similar to, but even more successful than, those recorded just before the battle of Fredericksburg, the armies remained motionless; and "no movement upon the Rappahannock" became added to the familiar notice —now as often repeated as a year before—"all is quiet on the Potomac."

POSTSCRIPT.

CHANCELLORSVILLE.

SINCE the foregoing pages were sent to the press, the public attention has been called once more to the neighbourhood of Fredericksburg, where a new contest has begun and ended, with a course marked by events as interesting as any of those previously recorded. The purpose of the present chapter is to add to the former narrative such a brief sketch of the latest operations as can be furnished from the few reliable materials yet received.

The inaction spoken of at the end of the last chapter endured a full three months after Hooker had assumed command. So thoroughly shaken was the spirit of the Federals, and so unfavourable the weather to field operations, that Hooker appeared justified in merely holding his own, and striving to protect his flank and rear from Stuart's incessant attacks. This, indeed, he found a most difficult task with his inferior cavalry; and even the few miles of railroad which connected his head-quarters at Falmouth with Acquia Creek were not safe from the daring incursions of Fitzhugh Lee, who crossed the Rappahannock frequently in its higher course, and carried off prisoners on one occasion (25th February) from the very lines of the Federal camp. His cousin, W. Lee, was not less active below Fredericksburg; and by skilful handling of his light artillery, repulsed various attempts of the Northern gunboats to take advantage of the swollen waters of the river, and penetrate up it into Hooker's vicinity. With similar spirit and success, General Jones, who had been lately appointed to a new brigade of cavalry, and sent into the Shenandoah, protected that fine valley from the detachments of Milroy; for this latter general was now again employed in that district of Western Virginia where his brigade had before, under Fremont, won so evil a name. Jones almost destroyed the two regiments of cavalry attached to the Federal commander, by a surprise on the 26th February; after which he found no difficulty in sending his own parties down the valley, and even across the Potomac, on foraging excursions; whilst he managed at the same time to make detachments to his right across the Blue Ridge, to the frequent annoyance of General

Stahel, who had succeeded General Sigel — lately fallen under the displeasure of Halleck—in the charge of the district about Manasses. Another cavalry brigadier, Imboden, was no less active on the western side of the Alleghanies; and not only carried the war into that part of Virginia which had declared for the North, but threatened to enter the adjacent districts of Pennsylvania, part of which, indeed, his troops and Jones's did for a time occupy, in fugitive fashion, at the latter part of the spring.

Meanwhile, the main armies seemed motionless; and Halleck, either doubting the feasibility of a direct advance on the Confederate capital by any single line; or resolved to draw the enemy's attention from the real point of pressure; strengthened considerably the command of General Peck, who had for some time occupied and intrenched Suffolk, a town on the Nansemond River, one of the creeks which open northward into Hampton Roads. This place, only eighty miles by rail from Richmond, might at any time, it was evident, be used as a base from which to advance an army against that city by the southern bank of the James. Similarly, another such movement by the north bank might, at pleasure, be begun; by a reinforcement of the troops who had held the extremity of the peninsula ever since M'Clellan

CHANCELLORSVILLE.

abandoned it. Here General Keyes, lately returned to active service, lay with the advanced guard of the Federals at Williamsburg, and was observed by a small Confederate force under General Wise.

Threatened at so many points, and confident that Lee, with a less force than he had lately commanded, could maintain himself in the position at Fredericksburg, the Southern War Department divided his army considerably, by sending Longstreet, with three of his divisions, to take charge of the country south of the James. D. Hill was at the same time given a separate command, extending over all the coasts of North Carolina, where the Federals had another very considerable force lodged under Foster; and General Trimble succeeded to the division vacated under Jackson.

This detachment of Longstreet, and the bulk of his corps—for the two divisions he had left under Anderson and M'Laws numbered not quite 15,000 men—was not unknown to Halleck and Hooker. The forces nominally under the latter's command, at the end of April, reached the imposing total of 159,000 men, and a large proportion of these were massed round Falmouth. His information (derived through Washington, from secret sources) was perfectly accurate in assuring him that Lee did not command quite 50,000 men—infantry and artillery all counted—on the hills opposite; for Jackson's corps was at this time just 35,000 strong. Yet he could not choose to force a direct passage; for he had strongly condemned Burnside for doing so, in his evidence before the Committee on the Conduct of the War, and had charged that commander with failing through rashness; as he had also accused M'Clellan on the same occasion (for to throw blame on others he seemed to believe was to enhance his own merits) of ruining the peninsular expedition by timidity and incompetency. He formed a plan, therefore, in conjunction with the War Department, which, as to his own portion of it, and perhaps in its whole, has been somewhat, in the judgment of the writer, too hastily and violently condemned.

The project was, as far as Hooker's own share was concerned, to divide his army at Falmouth—now numbering nearly 140,000 men, in seven corps—into two bodies, for the purpose of distracting Lee's attention. The one should move above the fork of the Rappahannock and Rapidan, where the passage was comparatively easy from the division of the stream, and should cross both branches as rapidly as possible, thus debouching on Lee's left and rear. If he moved out of his entrenchments to meet them, the works would fall at once to the forces left at Falmouth; and they might be held, it was supposed, by a single corps when once occupied, while the other troops marched to reinforce the right wing. The latter would thus be strong enough, Hooker believed, to force Lee and his small army back; and, pressed by a superior weight in front, he would have no time to attempt to recover his works, and would therefore be driven to retreat, in order to preserve his railroad communication, the present head of which was at Hamilton's Crossing, three miles south-east of Fredericksburg. Should he attempt to take an obstinate defensive part in face of Hooker's right— and the tangled, woody country south of the fork certainly afforded much facility for rough entrenchments—the corps at Fredericksburg would act along the railroad, and intercept all supplies. In short, if the plan succeeded thus in its opening portion, *he must conquer in an offensive battle, or retreat southward.*

Whilst Hooker's army was to be thus employed— retaining with it only one brigade of dragoons, under Pleasanton—the bulk of the cavalry (now again commanded by Stoneman, who had left his corps for his old command) was to enter the country south of the Rappahannock by Culpepper, and having driven off the Confederate guard on that road, pass the Rapidan and divide into various bodies to cross the country towards Richmond, and break up the railroads in each direction, so as to prevent Lee receiving reinforcements or supplies. There was also an intention of strengthening Keyes' troops at Williamsburg, so as to quite outnumber Wise's, and directing the former general to attempt a forced march direct on Richmond, where there was known to be scarcely any garrison; but this latter part of the plan was never carried out, from some want of concert as to time, due to the Washington bureau.

Leaving these minor details out of our view, and regarding the project solely as it concerns Hooker's army, it will be seen that the basis of it was the fact that he could at first operate with two distinct forces, each superior in number to Lee's, and not therefore liable to be destroyed in detail. The latter general would almost certainly be forced to take the offensive against superior numbers, posted on difficult ground; and if he failed, would be unable to maintain his position between Hooker's wings. Thus forced to retreat, he would leave it open to them to reunite on the south bank, and press forward with their whole mass along the line towards Richmond. There is nothing, theoretically speaking, nearly as dangerous or difficult in what the Federals proposed, as in many of Napoleon's finest strategical manœuvres. But to carry out such conceptions as these, a general requires able subordinates, a practised staff, and well-trained troops; and Hooker's utter want of these essentials, coupled with his own inferiority to the opposing general, exposed his plan to miscarriage, and his army to defeat.

Towards the end of April the time had arrived—fraught with much anxiety to the Northern Cabinet—when numerous regiments of volunteers, raised in the enthusiasm caused by the fall of Sumter in 1861, could claim a discharge at the end of their two years' service. Many of these were in Hooker's command, and others in those which threatened Richmond from the south and west. It was necessary, therefore, to act at once, and on the 27th operations began.

Hooker's army at this time consisted, for practical use in the campaign, of the first corps, under Reynolds; the second, under Couch; the third, under Sickles; the fifth, under Meade; the sixth, under Sedgwick; the eleventh, under Howard; and the twelfth, under Slocum. Most of these corps, in their normal state, contained three divisions, composed of four weak brigades; but this arrangement was not complete in all. The brigades consisted of an irregular number of small battalions, and averaged less than 2,000 men in each. The whole distribution of the Federal army tended to a useless multiplication of untried and inefficient general and regimental officers.

The movement began by the departure of the right wing (Meade's, Howard's, and Slocum's corps), which Hooker led in person. The roads had been repaired, or made where required; and the preparations for bridging completely prepared, in a way that reflects much credit on that general's forethought for these matters. The troops advanced at first by the road from Falmouth to Culpepper, and crossed the Rappahannock, about four miles above its junction with the Rapidan, by the passage at Richard's Ford, and another farther up, called Kelly's Ford; then, turning southward, and still divided into two columns, Meade moving to the left, and the others to the right, they passed the Rapidan at Ely's Ford and Germantown, points on that stream about sixteen and twenty miles from Fredericksburg respectively. The two cross-roads they had chosen meet at a hamlet called Chancellorsville, twelve miles west of that town; and here they halted on the 30th, and awaited the arrival of Sickles' corps, and two of the divisions of Couch's, which Hooker, on finding

CHANCELLORSVILLE.

his advance as yet unopposed, had directed to leave the left wing, and move to join him by United States Ford and Banks' Ford. These are the principal places of crossing between Fredericksburg and the junction of the rivers; the former being just below that point, the latter farther down and five miles above the town. This last, being near Lee's position, was guarded by a brigade of Longstreet's old corps, under Wilcox; but the movement was safely completed by the other that day. Hooker had now united upwards of 90,000 men in his new position, where he passed the night—the army now fronting towards the east. Meanwhile, General Sedgwick, who had been left in temporary command at Falmouth, early on the 28th, threw bridges over the river four miles below the town, and crossed Wadsworth's division of the first corps, and part of his own, with but trifling opposition. He then made as though about to pass over the whole of the troops left with him, at that time more than half the army. But Lee was not to be so deceived. He had heard already of the westward march of the other Federal corps; and judging that Hooker meant to turn his position by outflanking it on the left, he kept his attention vigilantly directed that way, although he had not sufficient force to allow him to divide his army by detaching a part of it in that direction. As he expected, Sedgwick soon ceased his advance for the present, showing that the real passage was not to be made where he stood; and all remained quiet round Fredericksburg for the two days following, save for a trifling cannonade.

On the 30th, Lee had fully penetrated the main design of his adversary, and moved before dark to meet him; leaving in the works only the brave Mississippi brigade of Barksdale (which had defended the town against Burnside's first attempt at crossing), and half another brigade of the division of M'Laws. Opposed, as he was fully aware, to a greatly superior force, he could scarcely hope to obtain any very decisive advantage by attacking Hooker in front in so difficult a ground as that he was entering; described in one of his own reports as "a tangled wilderness." He made his resolution, however, at once, boldly and wisely, as the event has proved. With his two divisions of Longstreet's corps he determined to keep the enemy's front occupied for a time, whilst Jackson should make the circuit of the Federal right, and fall upon it with such a sudden flank attack as should prove decisive. To have thus separated an army already so inferior to that about to be attacked, and in its very face, would in an ordinary country, and with forces equally well led, have proved destruction. But the scene of action was peculiarly favourable to the concealment of such an operation; whilst in Jackson he had such a lieutenant to carry out his design as the world has never surpassed.

The morning of Friday, the 1st May, found Hooker preparing to feel his way onwards from Chancellorsville. Two roads lead from that place towards Fredericksburg, meeting, however, again in about three miles; and near the junction a branch road to the left conducts to the river at Banks' Ford. Meade's corps lay on this side of the Federal position; Couch was next to him, in front of Chancellorsville; Slocum more to the right; whilst Howard occupied the right rear and the roads from the Rapidan; and Sickles was held in reserve. About 9 A.M. a slow advance was directed by Hooker along both roads. Sykes, whose division of regulars formed the advance of Meade, soon came into collision with a Confederate brigade, and much skirmishing ensued without any progress on either side. At about 4 P.M., Slocum's men were sharply attacked; and later in the day, the Confederates again took the offensive still farther to Hooker's right. In fact, Lee was at this time employing Anderson's division in detached brigades along the Federal front, with a view of fixing Hooker's attention on that side, and covering the movement of Jackson. These attempts were so well managed as to deceive the large force on which they were directed, and Hooker, in the evening, began roughly to intrench his position. He also sent orders to Reynolds' corps to leave Sedgwick, and join him by United States Ford; which was done at once, and raised his immediate command to more than 100,000 men. It seemed that already his usual courage was giving way beneath the weight of his responsibility; and this although he had informed his troops the day before of his great expectations of success, in those famous words, "The rebel army is now the property of the army of the Potomac."

The Federal work of entrenching—consisting, as usual, chiefly of making breastworks of felled trees—was continued through the night and following morning; and Hooker strenuously pressed on the design he had lately formed of remaining still and receiving the attack which he expected. But Lee, as we know, was purposely deceiving him as to its direction, and continued on the morning of the 2nd to repeat his demonstrations along Hooker's front, his brave troops—still chiefly Anderson's division—in many instances carrying their assaults much farther into the Federal lines than he desired, and losing many of their numbers.

Meanwhile Jackson had begun with his wonted skill to execute the movement which crowned the brilliant successes of his life. Leaving A. Hill, as he went, opposite the extremity of Hooker's line to maintain his connection with the troops reserved by Lee, he marched the rest of his corps, about 24,000 strong, so rapidly on the circuit round the Federal right, that in the afternoon he had gained the road from Orange to Fredericksburg by the south of the Rapidan, which had been partly used by the Federals three days before in their advance from the Fords to Chancellorsville; and here he found himself undiscovered upon their right rear. He now deployed his columns north of the road, and then bore steadily down on the position of Hooker, which he reached about five P.M. So complete a flank attack on a large army has scarcely ever occurred in modern warfare, except in the instance of the Great Frederick surprising the Austrians, and "rolling up" their army by a similar march of his whole force at Leuthen, near Breslau, in 1757.

At first Jackson bade fair to meet with no less a success than did the bold Prussian on that memorable occasion, which gave him the greatest of his victories, obtained over 80,000 of the enemy by a force of barely 30,000 men. Howard's corps were not prepared by entrenchment or cover for an attack in this new direction, and their leading brigades, which were wheeled up to face it, gave way as soon as the Confederate shouts drew near. The panic flew through the others, and the whole corps fled in a rout so disgraceful as only the record of the first Bull's Run disaster can match. The German division, once formed under Sigel, made part of this corps; being now under command of Schurz, a noisy orator, whose "stump" speeches had led him into notice before the war, and caused him to be elevated to his present unsuitable position, as a sop to the Teutonic element of the army. His men were conspicuous in the flight, and bore even more than their fair share of the blame that followed. That Hooker's whole army did not suffer itself to be carried towards United States Ford, whither the fugitives bent their way, was owing to the precaution taken of leaving Sickles in reserve. Howard, a brave old soldier who had lost an arm at Fair Oaks, tried in vain to rally his frightened regiments. But Sickles, with his staff, succeeded in arresting some of the flying artillery waggons, stopping them by main force at the only opening in a wall which ran across the line of flight;

and by his personal exertion, and that of General Berry (who commanded his second division, and was killed in the struggle), turned the tide. His name deserves especial record here, for he seems to be the only one of the volunteer generals (he originally raised a brigade in New York) who has done signal service in the field of battle. Hooker was quickly on the spot in person, and strenuously resisted Jackson's further progress; and night closed the scene soon after this rally, the Federal army spending it in a much contracted position between Chancellorsville and the fork of the rivers not far off.

And now occurred an incident which entailed on the Confederates such a loss as would make any success dearly paid for. Jackson had left the scene of his immediate advance, and ridden towards his right to look for A. Hill's men. Coming suddenly on their front with his staff at about eight P.M., their horses caused them to be mistaken in the dark for a troop of the enemy's cavalry, and they received a volley, which killed one of the party, and wounded two others, of whom Jackson himself was one. He was borne off by a party of his anguished soldiers as soon as the truth was known; and A. Hill being almost immediately afterwards obliged to quit the corps for a time—for he was suffering from a flesh wound—Stuart was sent to command it. Quiet prevailed on that side during the night; but Hooker directed a night attack on those of Anderson's troops who seemed to press nearest to the Fords over the Rappahannock on the Federal north; and the object was attained by it of clearing a little more ground on his left front.

Lee did not allow the sorrow he felt at the news of his lieutenant's hurt to interfere with his sterner duties. Indeed a message from Jackson urged him to resume the attack at daybreak. This he did along the whole front of the Federals: on both fronts, it may be said, for their right—where Hooker had now placed Reynolds in relief of Howard—formed an obtuse angle with the line held by Meade, Slocum, and Couch, the two meeting just before Chancellorsville. On this point Lee succeeded in concentrating a number of guns early in the day, and fired a large brick building standing at the cross-roads, which Hooker had for several days made his head-quarters; ultimately driving the Federals before noon a mile beyond it towards the river. Here Hooker busily entrenched himself, and Lee pressed him no more for the present, for his attention was called in the opposite direction to his old position at Fredericksburg.

We left Sedgwick on the 28th with a part of his troops firmly established on the south of the river, just opposite the point held by the left of Lee in the battle of the 13th December. His wing was reduced, as has been noticed, by successive additions to Hooker's, until he was left on the 1st with his own corps only, and Gibbon's division of Couch's: but these gave him about 25,000 men. Informed (as we know from Federal sources) that the troops of Lee had vacated the whole of their works except Marye's Heights, and that the garrison of these—as his constant balloon reconnaissances assured him—was reduced to about 7,000 or 5,000 men (the real number was less than the lower of these estimates), he wasted his time in most unaccountable inaction. Whether he required more definite instructions from Hooker; or really feared, even with his great superiority of force, to face those entrenchments so fatal to Burnside's army; certain it is that his name must ever be discredited by the delay which ensued, when we know how well he was aware of the smallness of the rearguard which thus held him in check for four most precious days.

The firing about Chancellorsville, on the 1st and 2nd, told of serious engagements taking place there, such as should have urged him to make a diversion at once in Hooker's favour; and, indeed, it is evident that a few hours of exertion would have brought him upon the rear of the line with which Lee was deceiving an army already more than twice the strength of his own. Nevertheless, it was not till the evening of the 2nd, just at the very hour when Jackson fell on Howard, that he began very slowly to advance from his bridges towards the Heights. He wasted the rest of that day, and half the next, in crossing the four miles of ground which divided him from Lee's detachment. About noon on Sunday the 3rd, he prepared his divisions for a general attack on Marye's Heights; which being made on all sides, was far too much for the little garrison to withstand. The works were carried at once, with a loss of about a thousand killed and wounded by the fire of Barksdale's men, who kept up the contest until the Federals entered in overwhelming numbers. The latter captured nearly 800 prisoners and a dozen guns. About 6 P.M., Sedgwick, encouraged by the morning's success, advanced a column four miles on the road towards Chancellorsville, to a place called Salem Church.

But he was now too late either to reach Hooker, or to be of any use to him by separate action. That general was still strengthening himself in his position against any further attacks of Lee; and, it is to be supposed, was not aware of the small numbers of the latter's army, or that there were no reinforcements near. The Confederate general, on his part, had heard of the capture of Marye's Heights, and had despatched M'Laws to check any farther advance of Sedgwick's. The leading brigade of the latter was arrested at Salem Church by a rough breastwork; and the 95th New York Regiment, attempting to charge it, were mowed down by a heavy musketry fire, and fell back in confusion. This was enough to stop Sedgwick's corps, who were but feeling their way in dread uncertainty as to the real position of the enemy; and they halted, and spent the night between the heights they had captured and the scene of the evening's skirmish, their general line running across the road north and south.

Lee had resolved to deal with them effectually before Hooker should rally from his late blows. He drew that evening Anderson and one brigade of Jackson's corps from his late front, and directed them to make their way by cross-roads, and turn Sedgwick's left. So successfully was this done, that the next day, the 4th, had not far advanced, before the leading troops, Gordon's, which had passed round Sedgwick's flank completely, came out upon the old position of their army beyond the Hazel, and, advancing instantly, retook the heights, and captured a convoy which was moving after the Federal corps under a small guard. The other three brigades appearing soon after at different points of the broken ground which lay to Sedgwick's left, and M'Laws' men beginning also to engage his front with their skirmishers, he became thoroughly alarmed, and ordered his troops to move towards the right—the only direction which appeared open—in the endeavour to gain Banks' Ford. He was not severely pressed, for the surrounding troops were really less in numbers than his own, and were composed of brigades which had been continually fighting or marching for five days. He reached the river-bank early in the afternoon, and was not seriously molested until the evening, succeeding, in the meantime, in forming bridges with some pontoons brought to him by the north bank—for he had left some troops there, which now moved to his aid. About 6 P.M. the Confederates made a general attack upon two of his divisions, which were echeloned in front of the others. One of the New York battalions, the 20th, here gave way at once, and turned to fly from the shock, and its panic spreading from regiment to regiment—a Vermont brigade alone standing firm in the centre, and retreating coolly—the whole force fell back to the bridges with severe loss;

pursued by the enemy, until the latter were checked by the fire of some heavy guns, which had been planted on the heights of the northern bank. The same night Sedgwick succeeded in effecting the transport of his troops to the other side, not without damage from the shells which the Confederates threw from time to time among their panic-stricken enemies. The four divisions of the latter had been weakened by about 5,000 men, according to the admission of the Federals, among whom were many prisoners. Sedgwick moved westward next morning on United States Ford; but his force was in so shattered a condition that their accession to Hooker's army promised to be rather a burden than an advantage.

The same morning Lee, having thus effectually cleared his rear from the enemy, turned his attention once more to their main body. His active artillerymen were able, before many hours had passed by, to plant some heavy guns within long range of the Ford, and to throw shells among some waggons at its northern extremity. Another serious danger to the bridges at that spot was threatened by a storm of rain, which caused the river to swell so rapidly that the pontoons could hardly be held together. The day, however, passed away without any renewal of actual combat. Lee's troops most urgently required rest, and he contented himself with menacing the passage from a distance in the manner described, and with employing a few parties of riflemen to skirmish along the enemy's entrenchments, and keep up the impression that he was preparing to attack them.

Meanwhile Hooker, upon consultation with his chiefs of corps, decided to quit the position which he was now occupying without hope of honour or advantage. The difficulty of supplying his huge army, by a line of cartage running twelve miles along the north bank from Falmouth, and liable to constant interruption; the uncertainty as to the number of the Confederate forces, which might, for all he knew, be reinforced strongly from the south—for no news had been received of Stoneman's cavalry excursion intended to prevent help reaching them; the demoralized state of the army, of which the eleventh corps especially could hardly be trusted within sound of the enemy's guns; more than all these, the prospect of some flood, or some successful project of the enemy, destroying his bridges and reducing him to a state of blockade on all sides—these were quite sufficient reasons, in his view, and that of his lieutenants, to justify his instant retreat. As soon as it grew dusk, the preparations were made; and the sound being deadened by extreme precautions—as the covering the whole of the bridges with layers of small branches—the operation began, and was conducted with tolerable order. Meade was directed to line the entrenchments with his men, and resist any attack made on them until the other corps should have crossed. But the Confederates did not discover what went on; or if suspecting it, Lee's force was too small and too exhausted to be thrown away in night attacks on the chance of reaching the neighbourhood of the bridges, by carrying in succession the repeated lines of breastworks which barred the way. The crossing was effected before daylight, for Hooker had not with him any large supply of waggons, his circuitous march having forbidden encumbrance. The train having first passed over, the men themselves were marched to the bridges corps by corps; and in the early morning Meade's divisions were safely drawn in, and followed the rest. The campaign closed on Hooker's part by an address to his troops, which, in burlesque of truth and sense, surpasses the wildest bulletin with which Napoleon ever deceived the people of Paris. But the Federal general uttered his bombastic falsehoods without the excuse of their being useful in covering any part of his late errors or mishaps. He could not deceive his own beaten army; and for the rest, even the Northern reporters, writing under the supervision of his own staff, told a tale of disaster which all the world could plainly read.

Leaving the two hostile forces once more divided by the Rappahannock, it remains but to tell how Stoneman had occupied the time that had passed by. His expedition, though not of any practical value, was of singular boldness for a Northern cavalry officer. He left the lines of Hooker, just before that general began to move his corps, on the 28th April, with three brigades of horse, mustering 2,300 sabres. About one-half of these, under Averill, left Stoneman himself after the force had passed the Rappahannock at Kelly's Ford, and made for the Orange Railroad just above Culpepper, at that time occupied by Fitzhugh Lee. They drove in his pickets, and followed them up. Lee, whose force had been reduced by detachments to less than 500 men, abandoned Culpepper, and retired by Cedar Mountain over the Rapidan. Here he destroyed the bridge, and prepared to defend the passage; but Averill was content with what he had done, and having removed or destroyed the contents of a small Confederate depôt taken on Lee's retreat, he turned about, and rejoined Hooker by the same route that he had used in advancing, arriving at United States Ford just at the time when Lee drove the Federals from Chancellorsville.

Stoneman proved much bolder in his incursion than his lieutenant. Leaving the latter to occupy F. Lee, he moved his own command due south, and crossing the Rapidan unopposed some distance below the railroad, reached Louisa, a station on the Virginian Central Line, fifteen miles east of Gordonsville, on the 1st. Having taken up the rails in the vicinity, he pushed out various columns to carry the work of destruction in each direction. General Gregg with one of these made his course due westward, and arrived on the 3rd upon the Fredericksburg line at Chesterfield, where the railroad crosses the North Anna River. He spent that day and the next in following the line southward to a point beyond Ashland, a station only fifteen miles from Richmond; destroyed on the way three considerable timber bridges, and captured a train bringing 270 sick or wounded soldiers from Fredericksburg, whom he paroled. Colonel Percy Wyndham in the meanwhile, who had been detached with a brigade from Louisa, took a southward direction, reached the James River at the town of Columbia, just south of Gordonsville, and having here cut a canal which carries the traffic along the line of the river from Richmond to Lynchburg, sent parties down the stream to another small country town, called Goochland, carrying off all the horses he could find, and as many negroes as could be persuaded to follow him. His force returned on the 4th to Stoneman, who on the 6th retreated northward, having left Colonel Kilpatrick, with part of Gregg's troops, close to Richmond. He having as far as possible, severed the communication between Fredericksburg and the Southern capital, left the vicinity of the latter by the Chickahominy, passed through the battlefields of the year before, and would have made his way by the peninsula to join Keyes at Williamsburg; but Wise, who had heard of the approach of the Federals, had detached a part of his force to await them on the line of the York River Railroad. Encountering these, and receiving a sudden volley from a party lying in ambush, they turned, and went direct on White House; and crossing the Pamunkey, followed the north bank of that river and of York River, until they reached finally the Federal post which occupied Gloucester, opposite Yorktown, where they were received, as may be supposed, with great surprise.

Daring as this raid of Stoneman's was—and his patrols on the 4th May were actually within four miles of Richmond, producing much alarm there—it will be observed that it exercised no influence on the struggle at Chancellorsville. Not only was the contest over when Gregg broke up the line, but there were no troops near Richmond that could be spared for Lee; and those to the south of the city do not appear to have been ordered up, so confident were the Confederate Government that Hooker would be defeated before they could possibly arrive.

Stoneman's operations showed, however, plainly that the Federals were beginning at this period of the war to appreciate and use cavalry in a way they had not hitherto done; and Colonel Grierson, on the Lower Mississippi, had about the same time, and in a similar way, found it possible to traverse the hostile territory as boldly as Stuart himself might have done.

There are some considerations yet remaining to be offered respecting the short campaign of Chancellorsville.

Making every allowance that is possible for Hooker's difficulties—admitting that his eleventh corps proved more untrustworthy in the field than he could have expected; that Sedgwick faltered painfully, and failed to second him in any degree; that he was under special difficulties as to the transport of the needful supplies for his troops—there still remains a degree of blame resting on his own performance of the self-elected duties of Commander-in-Chief, which nothing can hide, and which his own weak attempts to conceal by bluster render but the more conspicuous. It is only necessary to follow what has been said of his conduct from the time he was first attacked on the 1st May to the decision to recross the river, in order to see how completely the self-confidence of the man failed him in the hour of trial. Looking at the transactions here recorded in the most lenient view, he must be judged, like many another of his class—as a general, a fair leader of a division; as a soldier, a hard fighter, though too much of a braggart; but when raised to chief command, a man utterly incompetent to the higher duties of his station.

Turning to Lee once more, and reviewing his treatment of the difficulties that arose during Hooker's advance, there seems literally no praise too high to bestow on him for what he did with his small army in this brief but glorious campaign. How he waited coolly till the movement of the enemy should be fairly developed; then by sharp attack checked his onward progress; then "contained" (as the phrase is) the main Federal army with less than two divisions, whilst Jackson performed that wonderfully successful flank march and won the victory; then, when he found the Federals reduced to perfect inaction, ceased to press them for a time, but still managed to observe them, while he transferred his blows to Sedgwick, crushing his corps with the lesser force, and driving him with great loss to fly across the stream; finally, contrived to keep Hooker and his 100,000 men so hemmed in and straitened, that they were glad to escape under cover of the darkness;—these things will have been observed by the reader, and carry the proofs with them, that Lee must be ranked among the very greatest of modern strategists beyond a doubt.

But lest it should be imagined that the Confederate chief has sprung, as it were, full armed into the possession of all the faculties which have given him a foremost place among generals, the writer would state his belief that no one has probably felt less surprise at Lee's recent triumphs than his old master in the art of war, the veteran Scott That general chanced to hold a conversation, not long before the war, concerning his campaigns in Mexico; and was charged in the course of it by a friend in the company with having, in the march which brought him before the capital of that country with barely 9,000 men, executed a feat so daring that he could not have conceived it beforehand. He replied, that he not only had conceived it, but had announced it, having explained it in the fullest detail to two of his officers; and that it was their conviction of the possibility of the enterprise which fortified his own judgment. "If their country should be in danger," he added, "those officers will prove to be great men." He named them; and one of the two is the present General Lee.*

The losses of the Federals in the campaign just reviewed, were, as usual, very variously estimated. But Hooker has admitted that his list of killed and wounded amounted to nearly 11,000 men. A great number of prisoners were also taken—certainly not less than 5,000; for 4,600 were sent from Richmond upon exchange within a fortnight after the battle. It appears, therefore, that the allowance of 18,000 made by the more moderate of the Northern journals for the reduction in their forces caused by the week's operations, cannot be very far from the truth. This number does not, of course, include some of the two years'· volunteers, who obtained their discharge and left the field with strange punctuality. One whole

* The writer is permitted to give this anecdote by a friend, who heard it directly from Judge Campbell of the United States Supreme Court, the person whom General Scott addressed.

battalion of New York Zouaves withdrew itself from Hooker the very morning following Jackson's attack! A Pennsylvanian regiment under Sedgwick behaved better, and voluntarily stayed for his first advance, sharing, of necessity, in the disasters that followed.

It is more difficult to say how much the Confederates suffered during the same period. It is certain that they lost more than 2,000 prisoners, including those captured by Sedgwick on Marye's Heights. The nature of their fighting being mostly offensive, and their men, in several instances, almost too freely exposed, their killed and wounded, especially about Chancellorsville, must have been very numerous. Lee's army may be safely considered to have been weakened by not much less than 10,000 men.

But their loss cannot on this occasion be reckoned in mere numbers. The death of Jackson, who sank under the effects of amputation on the 11th May, has left a void in their army which it will be hard to supply. Without taking too literally the words which Lee used on hearing of his wound, "It were ten times better that I were disabled than he!" we may assert that a great cause has seldom suffered more by a single death. But he has left his epitaph engraven in the history of the country he helped to create. His name will be cherished as long as that country exists. Nor can we doubt that such an example of pure patriotic valour and self-abnegation will call forth some kindred spirit to lead his troops on to further victories, and to complete that independence which he gave his life to maintain.

THE END.

www.ingramcontent.com/pod-product-compliance
Lightning Source LLC
Chambersburg PA
CBHW021938240426
43669CB00047B/422